T0167639

Samurai
WAR STORIES

WAR STORIES

TEACHINGS AND TALES OF
SAMURAI WARFARE

ANTONY CUMMINS AND YOSHIE MINAMI

The
History
Press

For Crystal, Austin and Claire – siblings who have
endured my interests for many years

ANTONY CUMMINS has a Masters degree in Archaeology and is the author of *True Path of the Ninja, To Stand on a Stone, Conversations with an Assassin* and *The Illustrated Guide to Viking Martial Arts*. He is a specialist on the nijutsu manuals of Japan, and has released several DVDs, as well as working as a host for the documentary 'The Ninja: Shadow Warriors'.

Yoshie Minami was born in Tokyo and currently lives in Saitama, Japan. She has a BA in Linguistics from the International Christian University. As a translator, she has published *True Path of the Ninja* and *True Ninja Traditions* and has worked with Antony as part of the Historical Ninjutsu Research Team on the best-selling *In Search of the Ninja* for The History Press.

First published 2013

The History Press
The Mill, Brimscombe Port,
Stroud, Gloucestershire, GL5 2QG
www.thehistorypress.co.uk

Reprinted in 2017

© Antony Cummins, 2013
The rights of Antony Cummins to be identified as the Author
of this work have been asserted by him in accordance with
the Copyrights, Designs and Patents Act 1988.

All rights reserved. No part of this book may be reprinted or reproduced
or utilised in any form or by any electronic, mechanical or other means,
now known or hereafter invented, including photocopying and recording,
or in any information storage or retrieval system, without the permission in
writing from the Publishers.

British Library Cataloguing in Publication Data.
A catalogue record for this book is available from the British Library.

ISBN 978 0 7524 9000 7

Typesetting, design and origination by The History Press.

Contents

Acknowledgements

A special thank you to Jackie Sheffield for her proofreading and preliminary editing, and also to Shaun Barrington, my editor at The History Press, for his continued support in helping to bring this and many other translations to life.

Author's Note

*H*istory – as I will repeat many times in my career – is best told by the people who were there. The samurai, while extraordinarily popular, are dramatically misunderstood. That is, people know what the samurai are, they know what they look like and they even have an ingrained pre-supposition of how they should act. However, this samurai image – which is one of Japan's biggest cultural exports – is a 'soft' image of the reality of the medieval world of Japan. Today's image is terribly oversimplified. This work will by no means correct this problem in its entirety, but will be more of a first step in revealing the real lives of the medieval knights of Japan. Embedded in a complex hierarchy and further subdivided by skills and tasks, an understanding of the whole of samurai culture takes an academic's devotion to understand. Therefore, to start to describe such a complex pattern, this text will separate out and display three main areas of the warrior culture of Japan. The first are the samurai themselves; the group of landed gentry – eerily similar to landed European knights – who are given fiefs so that they can provide war horses, gear, men and service in the name of their lords. The second is the ashigaru, or Japanese foot sol-diers, a group who have all but been brushed out of history. These lower class men were either conscripted, mercenary, or owed military service to a ruling family. A form of militia that were brought together for basic training and campaign duties, they make up the bulk of samurai armies and even venture into fully paid professional soldiering in some periods of history. Lastly, we consider the females of the samurai class, as seldom has there been an investigation into the position of the female in war. Three major Japanese texts have been brought together here to highlight these aspects of samurai culture and each will, it is hoped, help to develop a finer picture of a very exotic and mysterious world.

To understand medieval warfare is to begin to understand samurai culture. It is a preconceived perception that samurai combat is an honourable affair, with proud men on chargers calling out their family names and rank. However, this idealistic and simplistic understanding comes from great war chronicles, such as the *Taiheiki* text, which highlight the prowess of brave knights who have charged to their death. While this behaviour does indeed exist within the samurai class, it is only a small part of samurai warfare. In fact, betrayal, teamwork, hit-and-run, tactical withdrawal, assassination and all the facets of total war are found. Therefore, here you will read of the war deeds of both brave and cowardly samurai; read who beheaded whom; and learn all the skills needed to be an ashigaru foot soldier, or even how to decorate the heads of the dead if you happen to have the misfortune of being a female blockaded inside a castle.

Overall, this text is a foretaste of future translated volumes dedicated to the exploration of samurai warfare and the violent world in which they lived. Therefore, ignite the engine of the imagination and colour all of the mud, blood, smoke and flying banners that can be found among the black and white of this book.

Antony Cummins
Warabi
Japan

Information on the Three Historical Manuscripts Translated

ZOHYO MONOGATARI – THE FOOT SOLDIER'S TALES

With a possible three authors, this selection of tales is written from the perspective of the lower-ranking soldiers and servants of the samurai which is reflected in the syntax and tone. The purpose of this text was to teach lower-ranking soldiers the do's and don'ts of Japanese warfare through a collection of semi-fictional and semi-comical anecdotes attributed to imaginary warriors, and to deal with the very real needs of the battlefield.

The document can be dated and placed between two events, pointing to its origin somewhere between 1657 and 1684. In 1657 a devastating fire broke out in Edo called the Meireki-no-Taika, a disaster that this document refers to. Also, in 1684, a retainer of Matsudaira Nobuoki called Tashiro Sadaemon Tadakane referred to this manual in his writings, so it must have already beeen in circulation by that year.

The author or complier of these war teachings is unknown, but three people are often put forward as possible authors:

1. Matsudaira Terutsuna (1619-1671) the heir to Matsudaira Nobutsuna.[1]
2. Matsudaira Nobuoki (1630-1691) the fifth son of Nobutsuna.
3. Matsudaira Terusada (1665-1747) a son of Terutsuna and adopted by Nobuoki.

The first name, Matsudaira Terutsuna, was written in the postscript of a version owned by Mr Furukawa Hisashi. The second candidate, Matsudaira Nobuoki, is most widely believed as the author as his name is found in various versions in their postscripts, including the one owned by the National Archives of Japan; this one is presumed to be the oldest transcription known and can be dated to 1728. The third candidate, Matsudaira Terusada, is written in the postscript of the version owned by Tokyo University; however, he is widely considered to have been too young to have compiled these stories.

It is commonly said that this manual was meant as a textbook for low-ranking soldiers or servants. However, it was actually used for education by commanders of ashigaru or foot soldier troops for generations within the Matsudaira clan, and was transcribed repeatedly. There are various existing transcriptions of several dates (such as 1728, 1744 and 1776) but it was eventually printed in woodblock form in 1847 by Fujiwara-no-Kasuga Noriyuki.

The document consists of two volumes. Volume One has eighteen episodes and Volume Two contains thirteen episodes. The written form is a collection of tales from thirty imaginary individuals, including five ashigaru soldiers, twenty-five chugen, or servants, and a 'chief of servants', all of whom talk in turn about life in battle; this includes hints about their jobs, occurrences in battle, their masters and so forth. It was given in this form to help educate those soldiers who had not experienced actual warfare. The names of the 'story tellers' were constructed in jest; examples such as sunrise, sunset, big deep river and narrow shallow stream, are used in the ideograms that make up their names, lending to a light-hearted effect.

The writing style and syntax are constructed in a form that is meant to resemble the colloquial dialects of the foot soldiers of the time. This is quite pronounced, as most documents or manuals about warfare were,

---

[1]   Matsudaira Nobutsuna was the commander of the forces which defeated the rebellion of 1637/8.

at the time, written in a more formal style and, in contrast, can make the English translation appear base. However, terms like 'kick the bucket' and 'that bloke' fully represent the feel of the document, and the difference between Musha Monogatari – the second text in this book – and its educated audience is pronounced.

Overall, in Japan, the document is considered a very important manual and is thought to be a strong reflection of the happenings of medieval warfare, allowing this first English translation to be a cornerstone in understanding the world of the Japanese foot soldier and permitting us to see the world of Japanese warfare through its teachings.

Although there are a number of transcriptions existing for this writing, this translation used the printed version of 1846 as its major source. However, the last paragraph that mentions the fire of Meireki, in the chapter told by Koroku, is not included in the printed book but is found in the transcription kept in the National Archives of Japan. All the images used in this book are from the transcription kept in the National Archives of Japan.

THE MUSHA MONOGATARI – THE SAMURAI TALES

Written by Matsuda Ichiraku Nyudo Hideto in 1654 and distributed as a woodblock edition in 1656, this manuscript is divided into three volumes and records the stories of the samurai of the warring periods. From famous battles to small encounters, it was penned with the aim of preserving these war tales for future generations. Nothing more than the author's name is known of him, although it has been inferred that he may have been a monk at the time of writing as his name has connotations of a religious connection.

The manual is divided into three main areas:

Jo, or Volume One, which consists of thirty-three articles.
Chu, or Volume Two, which consists of sixteen articles.
Ge, or Volume Three, which consists of fourteen articles.

While these stories cannot be verified as wholly true in every respect and cannot be considered solid historical fact, they should be treated as general outlines to what was happening in the Sengoku Period and, like war stories of the Second World War, are still told two generations after the conflict.

Therefore, trust that the people and the battles contained in this manual are generally real but that minor details may have been embellished or altered. Above all, remember that they are based on the truth of a war that had not long ago ended.

The Tales of Women

The third and final section of this book includes two tales of separate women who were besieged in castles during the rebellions at the start of the Edo, or peace period; while short, they deal with the realities of battle from the female perspective and give us a great insight into the role of the woman during warfare in Japan.

OAN MONOGATARI – THE STORY OF OAN

Oan is not a name but is a title given to mean 'old nun' which makes this story the tale of an ageing nun, talking of her times spent within a castle siege. The author of this story was the daughter of a samurai who served Ishida Mitsunari during the Battle of Sekigahara in 1600. The writer was a later member of her family who had heard this story told by Oan or the nun when he, the author, was eight or nine years old. The story is of her experience in Ogaki Castle of the Mitsunari domain. After the fall of the castle she fled with her father to Tosa on the island of Shikoku where she married but had to be supported by her nephew after her husband's death. She is thought to have died in the Kanbun period (1661–1673) at the age of more than 80.

OKIKU MONOGATARI – THE TALE OF OKIKU

Kiku was a 20-year-old female who was besieged in Osaka Castle when it fell in 1615 and tells of her experiences, describing how she fled with a group after its fall. She later became the grandmother of a doctor named Tanaka Itoku who served the Ikeda clan. Kiku died in Bizen at the age of 83. The author of this text is unknown.

Both of the above tales were printed together in 1839 with a postscript written by Asakawa Zen'an.

Zohyo Monogatari, Tales of the Foot Soldiers, c.1657–1684

VOLUME ONE

鉄砲足軽小頭
Teppo Ashigaru Kogashira
The Musket Sergeant
By
Asahi Ide'emon

As it is my job to use the baton and conduct my men, I dare to state the following and I do so without presumption, so listen carefully.

I am sure I do not have to tell you this, but you should know that the main knot of your ration[1] belt should be in the centre of the back of your neck. Also, if the beads of the ration belt are on your chest it will prevent you from taking good aim with your musket.

Be sure not to shoot too quickly as people usually do at practice. You should pull yourself together firmly so that you will avoid meaningless shots and not waste ammunition. Remember, even after a gun battle begins, do not throw away your leather musket bag, this is a rule. Fold it in two, put two or three spare cleaning rods into it, then wear it on your back by putting it into any space somewhere on your right side. If worn too vertically, it will hit your headgear and thus be inconvenient. If it is placed horizontally, it would be dangerous as the rods may hit the eyes of your allies. Therefore, you should do as you think appropriate.

When the distance to the enemy is considerable, I will pass you a Hayago[2] cartridge, so you can shoot. If you are close to the enemy, take out a cartridge from your satchel. Warning: if you are hurried, it may burst open. Or if you handle the Hinawa fuse wrongly, it will not ignite the gunpowder and the fuse will go out. In the event where the Hinawa fuse has gone out, use another one; there are lots more Hinawa available, so replace it.

When a bullet is stuck in the barrel, a thick cleaning rod is put inside of another rod: use this and ram it down into the barrel. No matter how big the trapped bullet is, you can still load your gun.

---

1   They used to carry their ration in a form of cloth belt tied up into balls, each of which has rice for one meal.
2   A paper cylinder which contains a bullet and gunpowder.

While the men in the front line are shooting, those in the second line should set their Hinawa fuses. The target to be aimed at for each distance of 1 cho [109m] will be directed by us, that is, those who are in charge.

Even when you cannot see the enemy, you should not carry your musket on your shoulder without loading it. Always keep it charged whenever you carry it.

In case you shoot a mounted enemy, shoot the horse first then the man. However, it depends on the timing. Sometimes you should shoot the man first and let the horse run into the enemy's line and thus, disturb them.

When you get very close to the enemy, separate into the right and left groups and begin fighting with spears. When you have used up everything in your satchel, draw the cleaning rod from the waist, replace it with the musket and then draw your sword, cutting the enemy by aiming at his hand or leg. If you hit the front of the enemy helmet rashly, a blunt[3] sword will bend into a shape like that of the handle of a pot.

If you get to a good distance from the enemy, clean the inside of the barrel by wiping or washing it. In this case, be sure that half of the muskets should be loaded with bullets.

If you are out of breath after a lot of fighting, having just finished a tooth-and-nail battle, take out your Umeboshi plum from your ration pack and have a glance at it. Do not even lick it. Eating it is out of the question, but even licking it will make you thirsty. So keep it safe until you die. Remember it is just a medicine[4] for when you are out of breath, just take it out in such a case, but do not eat it.

In case you are still thirsty, even after having a glance at your Umeboshi plum, sip the blood of the dead or the clear layer atop of muddy water.

One Umeboshi will do for the entire period of battle. However, if you are using peppercorns you should take the same number of peppercorns as the number of the days of the battle you are, or about to be involved, in.

In summer or winter, crunch one peppercorn every morning, and you will not be struck by heat or cold. These are different from Umeboshi plums, as you will need a large supply of peppercorns.

3　The word here is used as humour and is a reference to the lower level swords used by foot soldiers.

4　A common understanding in Japan is that the body reacts to this sour plum with a watering of the mouth, thus stopping one from feeling thirsty.

Also, if you apply ground hot pepper[5] from your arse to your tiptoe, it will prevent you from freezing. You can apply it onto your hands too, but if you carelessly rub your eyes with your hand, your eyeballs will be bloodshot and a lot of pain will follow.

鉄砲足軽
Teppo Ashigaru
Musketeers
By
Yuhi Irizaemon

Since we are going to cross over the river, I will tie my satchel onto my neck. Also, the foot soldier named Hikoroku is such a strange man. He does not know how to wear his ammunition bag when he is in armour, so he was trying to hang the cord around his neck, like we usually do when we do practice drills again and again but he is doing this with his helmet-hat on (because we are in armour), but as the cord is too short to put it on in this manner, he should know that he has to cut the cord and tie it around his neck. He is so strange he does not know that the cord for the ammunition bag should be tied on to the breastplate of his armour. He is in no way a good musketeer.

Remember, the gunpowder in your Hayago cartridge is not only for shooting bullets but also for other uses. During this long spell of battle, we sometimes have to sleep in the fields or even in the mountains. Some may be bitten by Mamushi snakes. In such a case, put the gunpowder on where you are bitten to the amount of 1 momme [3.75g] and light it, the poison will disappear in no time, but it will not work if it is done too late. (See Fig 1)

5   *Capsicum annuum.*

弓足軽小頭
Yumi Ashigaru Kogashira
The Bowman Sergeant
By
Okawa Fukaemon

First of all, bowmen should always try to keep the knot of the ration belt at the centre of the back of the neck. If a ball (bead of rice) is on the chest it will touch the string, and you will not be able to shoot an arrow.

Before bow fighting begins, fix a Hazuyari[6] bayonet blade onto your bow. While the enemy is still far away, do not shoot the arrows in your quiver but the ones I give you. Once you get close to the enemy, use the arrows in your quiver. Never try to shoot farther than the distance you are told, but within that range or closer will be fine. Take good aim when shooting, try to draw your arrow back as far as you can as you always do at the practice marks. Be sure not to be spurred on and waste arrows. One archer foot soldier should be between two musket foot soldiers; therefore, shoot your arrows while they are loading their guns. You should not shoot arrows together with the two muskets. Remember, shoot in-between the intervals.

When the distance is getting too close to shoot arrows, position yourselves separately to the right or left side of the formation and keep shooting. If this is not possible, the best thing to do is to move to your left so that you can shoot the right side of the enemy, as the right side is difficult to defend.

As for a mounted enemy, shoot the horse first.

When you are running out of arrows, nock an arrow, do not shoot it at once but try to make the best of it by repeatedly pulling and loosening it, to avoid wasting it.

If the time comes you could be killed at any moment, so get close to the enemy, even closer than a spear's length and shoot the last arrow targeting a gap within the opponent. Then stab with the bayonet blade which is fixed to your bow at the enemy's face or any gap, such as an opening around the tasse – that is the skirt of the armour. After that, draw anything you like, such as your sword or your Wakizashi short sword, and try to cut the hand or leg of the enemy. Never try to hit the front of the

---

6   A spear-head or bayonet to be attached onto the top end of a bow.

helmet with your weapon; if it is poor in quality, then it will have the edge nicked and it will not function anymore.

It is tough and painful, but if you hang on to the enemy closely, there is a chance of you stabbing him with the short blade attached to the horn of the bow. All you have to do is cling on to him and stab.

弓足軽

Yumi Ashigaru

Bowmen

By

Ogawa Asaemon

When I restrung my bow yesterday, I happened to make a little crease in the string and with only one shot of an arrow did the string break. It was a well-made bowstring but it broke with only a little crease and thus it will not do for shooting anymore. It seems to be much weaker than an un-lacquered string. As it seems we are short of spare strings, I will have to restring carefully and so that I do not make this crease again.

The shaft of this bow is 6 shaku [6ft] in length, with rattan rolled at intervals of 1 shaku. Therefore, it is a bow to be used as a form of measuring ruler, the length of 1 ken [6ft]. If a ruler is in need, I can use this to measure things by placing it with the string downwards.

I think this one is a bow called the Shakudo Zukuri.[7] (See Fig 2)

槍担小頭

Yarikatsugi Kogashira

The Spearman Sergeant

By

Nagara Genzaemon

I think each of you need to have the following things in mind, but I dare say that just like a *sutra* for the Buddha or an iron rod for an ogre, the

---

7   Shaku is a unit of length (1 shaku is about 30cm), and Do means rattan. Zukuri means 'to be made with'. Therefore, Shakudo-zukuri means 'a bow made with rattan at 1 shaku intervals'.

following things are accepted as known by all though should be reinforced here anyway.

Remember to put the sheath for your spear inside of your breastplate before the spear fighting begins. A long sheath should be put on your waist, just behind your sword. For the front spearmen, be aware that the first people to attack should be samurai, so do not attack until they do. Also remind yourself that a spear is not only to thrust with. All men should work as one so that all the spearheads will be pulled together and in sync, and immobilise the enemy spears by striking them downwards. Do not take it for granted that you should stab with a spear. Thrusting should be fine in a combat with one or even two enemies, but if you have a number of spears, all you need do is to unite and strike down together.

For an enemy flag, use your spear to knock it down. If the enemy is mounted, remember to stab the stomach of the horse before the mounted enemy himself, so that he will be thrown down to the ground for you to stab him.

Once the enemy is in retreat, do not chase them farther than 1 cho, as it is not necessary.

It is better for us to stay together with the flags and Umajirushi standards for the general welfare of the army and do our best to defend those marks and be prepared for whatever happens.

Always be careful about the rivet of your spear and secure it firmly, so that it will not come off in an emergency. If it has a metal clasp, be sure to keep it tight by turning it around so that the rivet will not come off.

Concerning the Omochiyari Katsugi, or spear carrying servant – normally in Edo they get quite a stipend and walk at the front of a daimyo's parade, as they are carrying the most important weapon for a samurai. However, on the battlefield, the spears are the property of their masters and not for their own use, so they must not use them. On the other hand, Kazuyari are those lower-quality spears supplied by the lord, making them different from the above great spears. You can brandish or do anything with your Kazuyari spear, remember that there is no difference between you and the deeds you can do from those of great samurai. So, you should have strong hipbones and be well prepared so you will not fall behind.

To all Omochiyari Katsugi spear carrying servants – remember, if you use your master's spear yourself, it will turn out to be a thoughtless and cowardly act, so keep in mind that your aim is to carry the spear and not to fight with it; this is the best service you can do. Keep in mind the difference between these two kinds of spear services.

持槍担

Mochiyari Katsugi
The Spear Carrying Servant
By
Kichinaizaemon

While I was carrying a spear with silver fittings for my samurai master, I fell asleep and the silver Sakawa binding clamp on the spear end was taken out and stolen. Because of this I might be blamed and killed. Since I am to blame, I was hoping to do something fine by killing an enemy to pay for my blame. Then an enemy Musha came on horseback, and I thrust at the stomach of the horse with the spear and at full strength, almost like I was pounding rice into sticky Mochi, but as the binding was stolen before, the spear handle cracked. When I tried to pull the spear out, the end of the spear shaft stuck firm and came off, and was left in the horse's stomach as if it was being pickled in the horse's guts. The container of pickles was the horse's body while the 'pickling weight'[8] was the enemy. However, he did not fall from the horse's back and it turned out that I had the spear snatched from me − how unfortunate.

While I was thinking what I should do, by a turn of good luck, there came another enemy, who was carrying a spear with a hooked blade. The horse looked like it was just injured as its eye was bleeding, and it had been clipped by a spear, and he looked so undignified that I thought it would be really easy for me to defeat him. Thinking I might be struck in turn if I attacked him from the left side, I came at him from his right side, taking a grip of the spear shaft and aiming at the edge on the crupper;[9] I did this judging where it was best to strike, where it would not hit the horse's bones. I tried to pierce with force around the tuft of the crupper. However, the spear hit the horse [in the incorrect place, bounced] and flew about 5 ken away, and I slipped and fell down. If I had fallen holding the spear in hand, the horse would have run away, but luckily I let go of the spear when I failed [and by accident] it made the horse falter and collapse.[10] The enemy fell onto the ground facing upward,

---

8   When pickling, the Japanese would use a stone as a weight to hold the lid down.

9   A strap of leather which went from the saddle to and under the horse's tail.

10 This section appears to be a mistake, but the original is obscure and is not fully clear on why this happens. However, it appears he is saying let go of the spear when you have made a strike.

so I could cut off his head with ease as if he were asleep. The O-Wakizashi, or greater short sword, is so inconvenient for cutting off the head. There is a reason we wear a Ko-Wakizashi, or lesser short sword, on our armour. I was going to cut off this head, as if it were as easy as cutting the head off of a sleeping man, and while I was trying to do that – as the enemy was unconscious and hopefully before he came to – I sat astride him holding his neck with my left hand, trying to draw my O-Wakizashi again and again. However, the sash where the sword was fixed was loose, so when I tried to draw it, it came off halfway together with the scabbard. The blade of the O-Wakizashi is as long as 2 shaku and the scabbard had come out at least 1 shaku, so I had to draw the equivalent of a 3-shaku long sword with one hand, and I just could not manage it. In the end I twisted the blade so that it broke the scabbard and was finally free. This was very troublesome. If it had taken a little more time, the enemy may have regained conscious-ness and my head might have been cut off instead.

Modern scabbards do not have a Sakazuno[11] which is a small hook that holds the scabbard to your belt and that will not allow the scabbard to come off – people think it is cumbersome nowadays.

If my scabbard had one of these Sakazuno hooks, it would have caught the sash so I could have drawn the sword much more easily. I will knock a bent nail or any other such thing onto this scabbard now.

The sword and the Wakizashi and the spear (here around me) were the property of this samurai, though he is now only a head! And thanks to this head, my head can stay with my body and I am very happy about that. Over only such a small thing like silver fittings I nearly lost my life. I have heard old samurai say 'it is not good to provide armour or weapons with gold or silver fittings'. That statement is fair enough. Now I understand it totally. I have had such bad experiences due to the spear with silver fittings. I hear those who have such swords or Wakizashi with gold or silver fittings might be attacked by their allies while sleeping. The metal fittings of a saddle or stirrups, if taken away, will result, at worst, in shame. Therefore, gold or silver fittings on swords or spears are totally useless. They will cause big trouble! Though I thought that horse's eye – that I talked about earlier – was pierced with a spear and crushed, the truth seems to be that that beheaded samurai happened to hit the horse's

---

11 A small hook a short way down the scabbard of the sword to help secure the sword in place.

eye with his own hooked spear. Remember, you cannot have perfection in everything.

If you have a hooked spear, it can be advantageous sometimes, but it can be a disadvantage when you are on horseback. It depends on the situation if a weapon is good or bad.

数槍担
Kazuyari Katsugi
The Lower Spearman
By
Sukenaizaemon

Oh Kichinai, Kichinai,[12] you are carrying a hooked spear with a strange sheath on! What the hell is it?

Kichinai replies: This sheath was for my master's spear, but we were told not to throw away anything from our gear. If it is a short sheath you should put it inside the breastplate and, if it is long, then one should put it at the waist. So, I kept this old sheath for the master's spear and I fumbled around, trying to find it in my breastplate, but eventually I took it out and put it on this hooked spear as you see now, a spear I have looted by the way.

Also, looking at the other troops, it seems that they also have been told not to throw away the sheaths for their spears. I can see some spear-carriers carrying feather-decorated sheaths or even two-layered feather-decorated ones with the greatest care. Other chugen servants are carrying ones tied around their neck with rope. The funniest thing I saw was a spear carrying servant who was carrying a cover for one shaped like an orders notice board on his back.[13] I was laughing my head off and thought my sides would split.

These days people prefer a [decorative] sheath to help them distinguish themselves in a crowd, this is so it may act as an Umajirushi battle standard as well. Thus, big sheaths are commonly used, but once the battle begins you have to take the sheath off and the spear will

---

12   The nuance of the syntax here suggests that both of these people are of equal class.

13   The main point here is that the cover is nothing like the shape of the spear and is only for show.

be naked without it, therefore, it will no longer serve as a standard any more. If this is done it will result in not knowing where the general is and the spear carrying servants will have trouble with such a big sheath on their back. I have no idea why such large things are so popular these days. The spear sheath should be as simple and plain as a stick that is thrust out from a bush, this way is also better for the spear carrying servants. (See Fig. 3)

旗差馬印持

Hatasashi Umajirushi Mochi

The Commander's Standard Bearer

By

Magozo

When breaking into a run, I put the end of the standard's shaft into the leather support holder that I am wearing on my waist. However, when moving slowly, I will carry it and put it into the cylinder on my back.

Oh, it is so windy today. I will tie a rope onto the standard shaft and pull it to hold the standard upright. When the battle gets harder, all Umajirushi, or flag carrying servants, have to pitch in and join the battle with the enemy, then I will hit and swing away with the long shaft, if the enemy comes close that is!

馬印持旗差

Umajirushimochi Hatasashi

The Commander's Standard Carrying Servant

By

Hikozo

When marching slowly, it is better to carry the Umajirushi, or flag, in a cylinder. When moving very fast, it is more convenient to carry it in a leather bag which is worn on the waist. When you have to run even faster, I will roll up the flag and carry it on my shoulder.

In case you are breaking down the enemy's formation and the battle is getting hard, all flags or Umajirushi carrying servants should get together at one place and fight with the long shaft as a weapon.

As I was carrying two flags in the bag on my back, I have put one of the flags onto the flagpole now and will keep the other one in the bag.

Magozo says: I had two flags carried in my bag but now I have put one on the pole, but still one remains in my bag. (See Fig 4)

持筒

Mochizutsu

The Musket Carrying Servant

By

Tsutsuhei

Teppei, Teppei, I will not shoot the musket I am now carrying on my shoulder, as this is the gun my master is going to use. The ignition powder container will be dirty if I hang it from my neck, so it will be annoying for my master when he puts it around his neck. Also I think I should not always wear the leather box of bullets around my neck as the cord will also get dirty. Therefore, I have put them all together in a bag and tied it up at my waist. When the battle becomes hard, I cannot fight carrying the musket on my shoulder, therefore I will put the ramrod onto the inside of my armour and the musket on my waist, so I will be able to fight in this manner.

持筒

Mochizutsu

The Musket Carrying Servant

By

Teppei

Tsutsuhei, Tsutsuhei, you are quite right. However, the musket you are carrying is so small that you can carry it on the waist but the gun that I have to carry on my back is so huge that I cannot put it on my waist. On top of that, when I am given this musket back after our master shoots it, I cannot put it on my back quickly, well, not as quickly as you attach yours onto your waist. It takes me too long and I have so much trouble. Therefore, I think you and I should take turns to carry the big gun and the small one from tomorrow on? (See Fig 5)

持弓

Mochi Yumi

The Bow Carrying Servant

By

Yazaemon

You should be aware that a Mochi Yumi, or a bow, for our master is a totally different thing from the common Kazuyumi bow for the masses to use. Once the battle begins, I will give my master one bow and a set of arrows I have in the quiver. The other bow and set of arrows I carry are used if his string snaps or he has spent his arrows, so I must keep them on my back and keep them with care. Also you should not throw away the bow stand thinking it is of no use any more. Tie it onto your Jutsuuchigai ration bag with a 3-shaku long Tenugui cloth so that you can carry it on your back, which allows us to draw the swords on our waists and fight with them.

持弓

Mochi Yumi

The Bow Carrying Servant

By

Yaemon

As Yazaemon said above, it is totally different carrying a bow for your master from carrying a Kazuyumi bow for your own use. It is extremely foolish to shoot the bow for your own sake. Oh, also, I just remembered one thing and I will tell you what that is. Even though you are carrying a spare bow and arrows for your master, do not think at all that you should keep carrying them and hold them back. If you see another samurai who is empty handed, ask your master if you can give him your spare bow and arrows, if he says yes then we will have our hands free, that way we can freely draw our swords and fight. Yazaemon, what do you think? (See Fig 6)

草履取
Zoritori
The Sandal Carrying Servant
By
Kirokubei

Hey Yaroku, you used to carry the Hasamibako travelling box, but you have been told to carry a rattan trunk instead. On top of that, you are now carrying a sword. On the other hand, I have been told to carry some other burden as well as my regular task as a sandal carrier.

Yaroku, you have profited well because of this change, but you do not know how to wear a sword or Wakizashi short sword correctly; how strange it is, you wearing your swords this way! The great samurai people wear their swords and Wakizashi short swords on top of their armour, but they use a leather sword–belt called a Koshiate to make them firm. For people, such as me or you, Yaroku, it is really lucky to be allowed to be armoured. A leather loin cloth would be far more than we can expect. If you wear such a straight sword[14] as ours on armour, you cannot draw even a 2-shaku long sword with ease. If you wear them as I do, you can draw even such a long sword as 5 or 6 shaku. I will show you how to wear them now, like so; before you wear armour, put your sword and Wakizashi short sword inside your sash, then put on your armour as if putting on a Haori outer-jacket. As the country has been in a time of peace for a long period, we are not wearing our swords with the blade facing down anymore; this [way of the blade facing up which is now popular] is so we can draw them easily. So you do not need a rather sharply curved sword, ones so curved that they look like the handle of a pot. Also, curved swords hit your heels when you are walking; even great samurai or their retainers are wearing straight swords that resemble sticks [these days], just like the servants do.

If you put the sword under the outer obi [that is the sash outside of the armour], you will have a lot of trouble in drawing it, and if you try to draw when you see the enemy, it will only be half drawn out [as you are doing it in haste]. So, some people will try to finish this draw by holding the blade with the left hand but this is wrong as they end up cutting themselves, while others will just drop the sword and end up injuring their feet.

---

14   Literally 'straight' and 'sword' すぐな刀.

Because of the above, you will have to handle your Wakizashi short sword with one hand, but you cannot cut through armour with one hand and also the blade will break. This will leave you without and wanting, and you will not know what to do with your hands. I remember, there was one such person, who could not draw his sword, therefore he embraced the enemy with vigour, tumbling like a rice bag, up and over each other, tumbling around, which ended up with him being pinned to the ground. Next he tried to draw his Wakizashi short sword with intent and to stab the enemy from below but it had a huge gold-leafed guard, like a lid of a big pan – stopping him from drawing it. They used to say 'carrying objects that stand out on a battlefield is good', however this is not always good, in this case it prevented him from drawing his weapon before he was decapitated.[15] I have another story, another man who was also pinned to the ground had a big knife, as he was a cook and had a knife to chop vegetables and fish. So, he drew it out when he was pinned to the ground and stabbed it through the gap of the enemy's tasse, that is the armoured skirt about his waist. The cook then pushed upwards and wrestled the enemy over on to the ground and killed him by thrusting and turning the knife in his belly. The cook was the only one who was wearing a straight sword on top of his armour.

Also, you should remember, when you see someone on horseback draw their sword, they sometimes injure their horses as the tip of the sword hits the horse. Seeing these injuries, you may notice that curved swords or Ko-Wakizashi lesser short swords should be worn on top of the armour.

If you have a Ko-Wakizashi lesser short sword without a guard, you can draw it easily. Also, a large Kogatana – that is a big but slender knife kept next to the handle of your sword – has many benefits. You can use it if you have lost your Ko-Wakizashi lesser short sword or something like that. Therefore, Yaroku, remember you should not put a greater Wakizashi short sword under the outer sash of your armour. I took off my armour – just now – to show you how to wear it, but remember you should never take off the horse's saddle or take off your armour without our master's order. So I should put it back on immediately.

---

15   The original is being humorous at this point.

挟箱持
Hasamibako[16] Mochi
The Box Carrying Servant
By
Yarokubei

For my service for this campaign, our master liberated me from a Hasamibako travelling box, and he has had me carry a wicker trunk for him instead. Yesterday some Hasamibako box-carrier of another master was jostled in a crowd and had his trunk broken, so much so that all the things were scattered around and stolen. Moreover, as he slipped and fell, he was trampled on like a spider, making him vomit lots of blood. He then stood up and I heard he would have fought everyone then and there and to the death. However, it seems within their clan too, that fighting or any argument between allies is strictly banned, so he reminded himself of those laws and managed to stop his anger and kept an expressionless face, however, it was grudgingly and with shame.

Within our clan, any fighting or argument between allies is strictly banned, not only while we are in a battle camp but also whenever we are out on any form of travel. This is so because if you are not killed by the enemy when you return from the campaign, accompanying our master, you will be free to kill [anyone who has angered you during the conflict, as happened in the above story]. That bloke had dealings with those under another lord but managed to control himself; however, he did this with a sense of shame, but if he had grabbed someone and stabbed them in the belly, things would have depended upon the strength of his arm. Being a coward is also a no-no but he must have missed that, I guess.

However, it is a grave issue if you have not killed a single enemy but have killed someone on your side, even if they are not within your own clan — remember this is an insult to the honourable Shogun. Anyway, I suggest you should have as little contact as possible with those from other clans.

---

16   A travelling box carried at the end of a pole, which contains a person's equipment.

We are so lucky that we can have such a light-weight wicker trunk instead of the other heavy ones, thanks to my master's orders; besides we are also allowed to carry a sword. Now with this weapon we have a strong backbone, so much so that we could probably defeat the great and famous ancient warrior monk Benkei!

However, regrettably, the hilt of my sword was new when we left Edo, but as it is always in contact with the metal of my gloves, the braided threads on it have been worn out. Though once I thought I would die in my first battle, I now find that I have survived long and unexpectedly, and I feel my life will last long enough, so I am now at ease. On top of that, our master is a Hatamoto, or close retainer of the lord, and stays at the headquarters, which means we are far from the battle-front, so it is only sometimes we hear the sound of muskets. This said, we had a random shot come over to us yesterday and it weighed about 5 kin [3kg]. It hit me on the nose and bounced back leaving no trace.[17] So, no matter how much I think I might die, I just don't seem to be able to kick the bucket.

This worn-out hilt is a nuisance now I am still alive. Though I want to take it out and have a new one, there are no sword-smiths here, therefore, I am stuck and annoyed, though I thought such a hilt done like this would endure as long as I breathe; but now it has given me nothing but trouble. Oh, what should I do? Ah, that reminds me! You should not hold a Wakizashi short sword with both hands; instead you should hold it in one hand when fighting with it; because of this the hilt only has to be one hand's width long. As it is held in one hand it is better to be thin and should not be too thick. Thinking on, I think I should take away all the threads of this hilt and reduce it to the core.[18] Then I will hunt for some vines of honeysuckle or something else like that around here. I think I should put it into the hole of the tang and double wrap it. (See Fig 7)

17   The text here has a comical and mock-boastful feel. It is without doubt that this is an impossible feat and the point of this boast is to show humour and courage, as the bullet that hit him would have taken his head off.

18   The original does not say if this is back to the tang or wood of the hilt.

馬取
Umatori
The Groom
By
Kinroku

When accompanying our master in battle, there are essential things both of us, that is the two grooms, need to carry and need to know. First, you should attach the horse ladle[19] and the Hananeji nose twister onto your waist. Then put the headgear, the bridle and the bit around your neck. Also, hold the saddle-girth, martingale and the stirrup leather as well.[20]

Load the horse with the Mentsu, which is a wooden container for rice on the left saddle ring, while the small musket and the flag-holding cylinder goes on the right saddle ring. On each of the rear saddle rings hang bags of soy beans, and a satchel on the saddle horn, a bag of dried rice on the rear saddle horn and horse shoes on the rear saddle rings, so that they are fixed firmly. Always keep hold of the leash tightly and secure the horse to something. Attach the Kobanagawa nose-band onto the Tachigiki cheek piece to hold him in place and when you feed the horse, loosen and release the bit. As soon as the feeding has finished, re-tighten the headstall and bit the horse again.

When you hold the horse still, even for a little while, be sure to put the hobbles – which is a form of mesh net that goes around the knees – on the legs and be sure not to let the horse go. If you let a young horse loose, it could cause a big commotion, so much so that it may turn out that we lose the battle. So never fail to check and restrain the horse with the rope tightly.

Also, I tell you this just in case you need to know. The Mozuogane metal fittings which are on the stirrups sometimes break and we do not have spare stirrups to replace them, so in that case, be aware that you have to fix the stirrups by tying them up with anything you can find.

A blanket should be kept on the saddle when the master is mounted. Do not throw it away, this is so that the master can use it as a mat. The under-blanket can be used for us footmen as a mat when needed. Remember you should utilise every item in your gear with great care.

19   The Mabishaku 馬柄杓 is a ladle used to wash the horses.
20   The idea is to hold the head gear for the horse tack around your neck.

馬取
Umatori
The Groom
By
Toroku

Kinroku's above story has reminded me of something. As early as within seven days of my birth, I heard my great grandfather, Hikozo, say the following and I have kept it in mind for the last twenty-four or twenty-five years now.[21] I remember, he said someone had a mouse on a leash which was tied around its neck, but the mouse escaped and one or two military units at first made a fuss of its escape. Then that fuss caused a bigger commotion, and made other people think that they were under an enemy attack, which in turn brought about the collapse of troop after troop as they fled in fear. Those in the rear troops tried to stick to their positions, however if the ones in the vanguard are as small as dwarfs and those in the rear are as big as the Great Statue of Buddha, then once an army begins collapsing there is no way to stop it.[22] Grandpa Hikozo also told me that they were all shouting in fear and a massive army of 50,000 to 60,000 people ended up withdrawing as far as a ten days' distance, all at once. So I remind you that it is quite reasonable for Kinroku to encourage you to restrain a horse as much as he did in the above story. As even with only one mouse, things went thus. Imagine if a horse was released, it is four or five hundred times as big as a mouse, this means that the same army as above would have to withdraw by 1,000 days distance. That would be even more than going through the whole country from the tip of the west all the way to Ezochi[23] in the north, it would be quite something to see. Therefore, army protocol strictly tells us not to release a horse, so we must handle horses most carefully.

Along the same lines, you are not allowed within the battle camp to sing a Kouta ballad, recite a Joruri dramatic recitation or storytelling; this is set with the aim of preventing us from raising our voices

---

21 This impossible idea, that he could hear and understand at seven days old is humorous. The specific time comes from the Japanese celebration, the Shichiya, which is held seven days after a child is born.

22 This sentence has an element of comedy and implies a 'mock reverence'.

23 The original name for the island of Hokkaido.

in cheer. It is for this reason too that something called a baiboku[24] mouth gag is used.

It does not seem likely that all of the 50,000 or 60,000 people at that time were cowards, and some people must have been brave and composed; however, even though it was only one or two who made a fuss at the beginning, once it had turned into a big commotion, it seems to have been very difficult to contain. So remember this, never let go of a horse!

This is how to hold the bridle:

If the master holds the bridle and takes command of the horse, we grooms have our hands free and nothing to do, so it is a shame if we do not kill the enemy, for we are now wearing swords!

Also, from my experience of serving forty or fifty different masters, it depends on the clan how you should be prepared mentally.

Now I am on the battlefield serving a samurai master and I have realised that, though samurai often talk about being killed as the result of their feats in war, I say to you my friend Kinroku, there is not such a great chance of being killed, if I am honest that is. If you are killed for nothing, the enemy will be highly spirited and at an advantage while your allies will become panicked and in a disadvantageous position. If you cannot help but be killed, then at least try to kill at least one enemy if you can. Of course, killing two makes it an advantage but to kill as many as 100 would be best if you can do it. This all depends on the strength found in the sinews of your arms, if you waste your life without killing anyone, it is surely a cowardly thing to do. If you die for nothing, the rations you have been given will also be in vain, so always keep this in mind.

---

24 Baiboku – a form of wooden gag held in the mouth to keep troops quiet.

沓持

Kutsumochi
The 'Shoe Box' Carrying Servant[25]
By
Kichiroku

As I am allowed to carry a shoe bag on my back instead of carrying a trunk, I can move freely in battle, so much so that I could even beat the famous warrior monk Benkei. On top of that, I am wearing a sword on my waist – I feel I can do anything. However, on deeper reflection, I am aware that my most important job is to take good care of the horse so that it will not get tired, this is more important than anything I could do in battle.

This horse was engaged in close combat fighting this morning, chasing or overtaking for about one hour, and the enemy were driven away in the end. Since the horse really has done quite a hard job, I want to feed him as much beans or porridge as he likes. However, it is not good to feed him too much at once. What I should do is let him eat little by little and do not let him lie down at night but keep him standing up. If he lies down, he will be tired and useless tomorrow.

Also, when I see other shoe carrying servants from other clans, they seem to have a lot of trouble. I mean if you hold a trunk on your shoulder, you cannot do anything, even if an enemy comes to behead you.

When we were last on the march, a horse belonging to another troop became excited, so much so that the footmen and the rider were trying hard to calm it down, but it would not be still and made the horses around him excited. Then one shoe box carrying servant was stuck between some horses and was trying not to be kicked by them in the confusion. It turned out that his trunk hit the hip of a horse and that made the horse even more excited, making it further out of control. On top of that, he fell down and the trunk was totally destroyed in this muddle. As we have free hands, because we carry bags, I will do anything to help my comrades Toroku and Kinroku if such a thing happens to them. (See Fig 8)

25   A servant who would carry footwear that is not Zori sandals.

VOLUME TWO

矢箱持
Yabakomochi
The Arrow Box Carrying Servant
By
Yazo

Until yesterday, we two soldiers were carrying a burden of 100 arrows each, but this morning a skirmish of 200–300 people began and now it seems that we will run out of our supply of arrows. We cannot get the packhorses, who have the arrows, to the front of the column. Each of us has been carrying a box with 200 arrows, instead of loading them on the horses. This is because the battle has been carrying on since this morning and now my guess is that everyone is running out of arrows.

Oh, also, I just remembered one thing. I saw two strange people among the ashigaru foot soldiers; this is what they did:

Seeing the enemy were at a distance of about 10 cho away, one of the ashigaru became flustered, thinking it was the distance we were told to start shooting arrows. Even though the gun shooting had not started yet, he began shooting arrows and used up all in his quiver. When spent, he was totally out of arrows but had not succeeded in killing a single enemy, he had nothing he could do but call out to us for supplies, his voice rang out, 'Yabakomochi![26] Yabakomochi!' However, he found that there were none of us around, so he began contemplating about what he could do with a bow, even thinking about throwing it away, as now it was as useless as a stick, but then he remembered that he had fixed a Hazuyari bayonet blade on the tip of the top of his bow. Just then, an enemy attacked him with his nose hair sticking out, that is to say, with his guard down. So aiming well at the enemy's nostrils he stabbed with his Hazuyari blade – which is the bayonet on his bow – and it pierced through his face and out of his earhole, and as a result he claimed one head for his collection.

---

26   This is their job title.

34

The other strange ashigaru that I saw before looked so pale that I thought that he may be terrified. He had shot all of his arrows but one and regained his composure,[27] so much so that he could remember what he was told by the protocols laid down by the army. Thinking he would shoot his arrow at the last moment of his death, he took the arrow, nocked it to his bow string and kept hold of it by drawing and loosening his bow for a 4 or 5 cho distance as he moved, waiting for the correct moment to actually let the arrow fly. Just then an enemy came to him, charging with his mouth wide open like a crocodile, at this, the ashigaru with one arrow waited until he got as close as within a spear's distance and when he came as close as staff length,[28] he shot the arrow, which pierced the enemy through the mouth to the nape and into the back plate of his armour. At which point the enemy fell down to the ground face-up and the bowman beheaded him. His early performance was poor and if you reflect on it you can see it was totally a waste of arrows as his shooting was for no reason. Think, if even one arrow is enough for you to achieve such a feat, you must understand that it is not a good idea to keep shooting from the beginning of the battle and exhaust your arrows. The same thing sometimes happens with the samurai. Some samurai do not think us chugen or komono servants – those like me and you – are worth much and treat us roughly at first. However, if the servants bark back at the samurai like dogs, they will show their weakness and in the end their shame. A common saying goes, 'Rudeness blooms out of cowardice, that is to say cowardly dogs bark loudest'; this is the same thing.

Of the two ashigaru I mentioned, the one who killed his enemy with the Hazuyari bow bayonet and the other who killed with an arrow, I think the arrow story should get more credit, if talking about which feat is greater. I think this because the first ashigaru had used up all his arrows, which is not a good thing to do as a bowman, even though he got a head. What do you think?

I have kept this staff that I am holding now, because it will be useful when we have to carry any two arrow boxes or bring water, as you know.

---

27 This sentence is loaded with humour that does not translate into English, it implies that he has accepted his death and is ready for it.

28 Usually 6 shaku long.

Well, well, guess what, we have done better than getting a head! That is because we are carrying out our duties very well and it is worth more than killing with a Hazuyari bow bayonet, like the one I just talked about.[29]

When I picked up a spent arrow and had a good look at it, I found the arrowhead was not held very tightly and had come loose, and the head and shaft broke apart easily. Because of this, I will fix the arrowheads, that are in my arrow box which is on my back; I will secure them very tightly, that is before I give them out. I must say, it is miserable to bear an arrow box on your shoulder, as we used to do; you could not move without some difficulty. Now we are carrying it on the back like a backpack, it is much easier, so much so that we can rush around as much as we like. Which reminds me, when we crossed the mountain yesterday, did you see other servants carrying arrow boxes in other troops as they climbed up? Each load was carried between two people but the front corners of the boxes got caught; this meant that they had much difficulty when carrying them up. They tried to lift them with so much effort that someone ended up falling down the slope and the arrows were scattered all over. On top of this, the people passing by them were treading on the arrows so that all of the arrows broke and there were none left fit for use. Since we are carrying the box on our backs, we can climb up and down such a mountain as the one yesterday, as many as 100 times for the same period of time that they were struggling.

玉箱持

Tamabakomochi
The Bullet Box Carrying Servant
By
Zundon[30]

These bullet boxes, which we two were carrying with a pole together, have been held separately on our backs since yesterday's skirmish. Now in the battle, I hear the sound of the ashigaru troop shooting their muskets: it is like that of scrubbing a straight spear with a grass ball.[31]

---

29   i.e., they have been respectful and carried out their jobs without interfering with the combat.
30   Onomatopoeic, the same as the sound of shooting a musket.
31   The reason for this is unknown; a crackling sound perhaps?

Normally, if the bullets are carried in a satchel on the waist for a long time, then the gunpowder in the Hayago cartridge is wet and stiff, and people put these cartridges straight into the musket and shoot. This means that some gunpowder is left unused at the bottom of the cartridge and the bullet does not go as far as 5 ken – which is a very short distance – but just drops out of the end of the gun and rolls around.

Therefore, you had better shake the cartridge before loading it into the gun. On top of that, when putting gunpowder into a cartridge, you should not pack it to the full but leave a little room. If you apply too much glue on the paper to cover it, the bullets will be stuck onto the paper, almost like it is wearing paper clothes, and sometimes the paper will not break. That means that after shooting it two or three times, the bullets will get stuck in the barrel and when you put a cartridge in it, it will only reach 2 or 3 sun [1 sun equals approx. 3cm] down the muzzle – which is not far at all – and then if you try to remove it by thrusting it with a cleaning rod, it will get stuck and you will not be able to budge the blockage an inch. You cannot get it to go deeply into the barrel, even if you beat or hit it. And so, if you shoot it as it is, the bullet will reach only 4 or 5 ken ahead, making the musket worth less than a mere stick. Even those bullets that are not covered with glue, small ones will go deep down the barrel, but when shot they only manage to reach 4 or 5 ken again. This means that hordes of bullets, gunpowder and cartridges were spent for nothing – what a waste!

Tapeworms are going around these days and they are even more common in a battle camp; many people suffer from them, making people even more flustered.

I will tell the ashigaru troops about this next point! If the bullets are too small, you should bite them with your back teeth before you use them and also remember to take good aim, then it is ok for you to use up all the bullets in your satchel at once if you have a good aim, but if you shoot at speed and just waste the bullets? As orders go, with arrows or muskets, you should take good aim at the enemy and release very calmly. By repeatingly loading and shooting their muskets quickly without break, they wasted bullets and gunpowder by shooting in 'rapid fire', without killing a single enemy. What a shame it is!

Now I gave out all the spare ramrods I had on my waist at first, which means I am burdened with empty leather sheaths and an empty bullet box. An arrow box can be used as a water bucket while this bullet chest can serve for nothing else. I want to throw it away, but it has been left in my keeping so I cannot. I have no sword, the burden is so heavy and the empty box is useless, my job of carrying the bullet box is not so good as the ones carrying the arrow boxes at all and I envy them.

There was one ashigaru who used up all the bullets and gunpowder in his satchel. He then took out the ramrod and put it on his waist, drew his sword and struck an enemy on his helmet and the sword bent, so he then drew his Wakizashi short sword and stabbed the enemy in his stomach. Just while he was going to take the head, we had an order from our lord to withdraw. He was half way through the beheading but we were told to get back right away, so he had to give up and leave the head. This means that he had his sword bent and had abandoned a head as well, this must be a great disappointment to him. However, the troop commander said he would guarantee his feat so it is almost as if he had taken the head, this is good proof indeed.

During a skirmish this morning I saw a strange person carrying spare bullet boxes and advancing on my left side. As the fight between ashigaru foot soldiers was getting hard, the samurai in the rear became intolerant and came to battle. The servant tried to get to the side, as the ashigaru group moved to the side at the same time, but he was carrying two bullet boxes on one pole and over his shoulder so he struggled and fell and got stuck; this meant that he could not walk any further but was stranded. Eventually, he could not catch up with the ashigaru group and became totally panicked. However, at least he was lucky he was not stripped of his bullet box. Remember, as we are now carrying our bullet boxes on our backs we do not have such bad experiences – how wonderful this is. (See Fig 9)

荷宰料

Nizairyo

Quarter-master

By

Yagi Gozo[32]

What a massive horde of people! We've been advancing for ten days but we have not finished yet. It will last for another ten days. We, with a group of packhorses, are far behind our troops and we cannot catch up with them. Each man in our troop has rations for four or five days in the ration bag around his neck, so if we cannot get our horses to catch up for three or four more days, they will not run out of food. Whether we are in the enemy's territory or not, you should not let your guard down, even with your allies, as they may rob you of your food as well. In such a case as this one, when rice is getting hard to come by, then even allies start robbing each other. Do not let your guard down or you will be robbed. Now we have two pack horses free from their loads, so remember not to throw away even the pack ropes or round straw lids that are at each end of a bale of rice. The ropes are made of dried stems of taro, stewed with miso, and twisted. This means that you can cut this rope into pieces and put them into water, this will make solid ingredients for soup if you need it. The straw lids of a rice bale can be used for porridge for the horses, so keep them with you for sure. Once you get in the enemy's territory, obtain whatever you find and can get without question. Suppose you are in a famine while in battle camp. As well as any edible seeds or nuts you should take anything like roots or leaves and put them on horseback. Pine bark is edible if you stew it into porridge. Sometimes, the rice that is around your neck in the ration pack is still in its husk, and when it is soaked from heavy rain or river water it can put forth shoots; wait until the rice grows to the size where you would normally plant it, but in this situation stew it together with its roots, this will make a good meal.

80 momme of firewood is enough for each person, if the amount for all is put together, it will make a good fire. In case you are running out of wood, use dried horse dung or anything for fuel.

People usually bury rice or clothes within their house. If they bury them outside, they put them in pots and kettles and cover them with soil.

---

32   The name is a play on words to do with his position regarding food supply.

On a frosty morning you will see the frost disappear on the ground where they bury the goods and you can find them. However, if days have passed, you will not be able to see them as this works only immediately after they have been buried. Keep this in mind and dig them out.

You should not drink water from a well in the enemy's domain. They usually throw shit into it so you will have a stomach-ache. Drink water from a river. Still water from a strange land may give you diarrhoea or stomach trouble. Be sure to take apricot stones with you and remember to pack them inside cloth, put them into a pot and boil the water. You can drink this water. Also you can dry 'river snails' from the rice fields of your homeland by leaving them in the shade,[33] and boil them with water, so you can safely drink it.

夫丸

Bumaru

Labourer

By

Bazo

Gozo-dono, Gozo-dono, you are right, we always have famine in a battle camp. What you have said sounds fair enough. As well as the great samurai people, you too are armoured and wearing a long and a short sword, looking dignified. However, you might not know about how to sustain your whole body during the battle camp as well as I do. I used to carry salted vegetables from my land to Edo every single day, in summer wearing a worn-out kimono or in winter stretching the sleeves of my cotton kimono to cover my hands. When it snowed, I took an old used rice bale and put a hole in the centre at the top and wore it with the brim around my neck, along with a torn straw hat on my head. In that outfit, I would walk back and forth for two or three days, both day and night that is mind you. I could not feed the horse the required amount as I only had a little bit of bran in a bag, so sometimes the horse was not fed for a while, well, on nought but water anyway. However, you and the great samurai look so dignified in battle whether it is hot or

---

33   It is still common practice to dry objects in the shade in Japan as the direct sunlight is considered too hot.

cold, whether you feel weary or sleepy, and you people may not have as much knowledge as I do about how to keep up your body in such harsh conditions. The first thing you should keep in mind is, do what a beggar does to preserve your body!

Gozo: Bazo, Bazo you are quite right! As I was worrying about what you said above, so I have brought my Nunoko quilted long jacket and I am wearing it with its bottom tied up, but I have taken it off as I was so hot and I have put it into an empty rice bale.

Gozo-dono, Gozo-dono, I only hear you talk about battlefields, in the mountains, near a river or in a field, but what if you have captured an enemy castle and have to stay there and defend it? I am saying this because, though I am ashamed to say this, I used to be a samurai and have fallen to being a peasant, just as you see me now. My grandfather's name was Bahyoe and he would always tell me, 'when they were in defence of a castle, they would save the most important things, like food, animal feed, arms, but also stone, wood, or anything according to their uses, but the most essential thing was a water supply.' My grandfather Bahyoe happened to be holed up in a mountain castle and they were seriously in need of water and thought they were dying as they were completely parched. As water is enormously important, you should estimate one Sho of water for each person. For food and such there is a rough indication for these things, for example, six go [1 go =180ml] of rice for each person each day, 1 go of salt for ten people and 2 go of miso for ten people. In the case of a night attack, an extra amount of rice was needed.

Remember, if quite a large amount of rice is given at once, boozers would make sake wine of it, so you should give only three or four days the amount of rice needed at most, but not any more than five days' worth.

I just wanted to let you know this in case of the need to stay in a castle for defence, as these are old ways that were actually used. What do you think, Gozo-dono?

Gozo replies: As you say, Bazo, if you give ten days amount of rice all at once, boozers will no doubt make sake of eight or nine days worth and drink it up. And in this case they will die of hunger. Whereas, if they drink sake made of three or four days the amount of rice, then they will be able to go without food for two or three days, this is acceptable.

In a Joruri story book titled *Azuma Kagami*, it says that in old times, an army sent by Lord Yoritomo marched from Kanto for the Western lands and were in serious need of food on their way and sold their armour and helmets to gain it. With that money they bought and ate rice, and then led an assault without armour. If you are wearing armour but have no food, you could in no way distinguish yourself in war. In short, be patient like a tramp or vagabond while in a battle camp. For dying in combat is what we want but if you die of hunger due to the lack of rice, without fighting the enemy, it would be no better than a tramp's death in the gutter and all would be for naught. (See Fig 10)

若党
Wakato
The Young Followers[34]
By
Sasuke

Well, well Kasuke-dono, you did a good job. You did even better than the samurai as a Yariwaki[35] aide, when backing him up in a spear fight and you also got a head! Thus, not only your master but also you, his retainer, achieved a great feat.

I have brought this cloth as a band to hold back my sleeves in case my master gets injured and I have to carry him on my back secured with this cloth. However, my master got the honour of the second spear achievement and yet remained totally unscathed. He had his comrades back him up with the sword as a Yariwaki support. By the time of the third spear match, all the spears from both sides of the enemy and our allies were crossed together at once and there were so many spears tangled that it was messy like salted bracken,[36] a great mix. My master was in the second match and I saw your [Kasuke's] master striking the first blow of combat with you backing him up. It really was a great achievement that you and your master made! So did

---

34   Lower class people who fought, literally 'young group'.
35   A support person who helps someone fight – a man at arms – the main combatant has a spear. So first spear (Ichibanyari) and second spear (Nibanyari) are those brave enough to fight the enemy first. After these two attacks these side supports who fight off the enemy are no longer needed as mass combat has ensued.
36   Bracken was salted in boxes, its straight nature is used to represent spears in this case.

my master, who was in the second match. It has been said from olden times that the first and second person to enter battle are great and that the third is of no importance. After the second person, every spearman in the troop makes an assault and all at once, so there is no need to back them up with Yariwaki support troops, so forgetting about these Yariwaki support people, think of the following problem. I was pushed and hustled badly when the two sides clashed and I had the strings of my armoured skirt torn off. Black armour looks brilliant, but black strings or anything dyed black are not good for armour in general. I have brought some leather for fear that the strings of my armour might snap. I will mend these skirts with this leather. I have noticed that you are injured badly but pretend not to display any fear, that is what I have observed anyway, though you always have a good complexion and appear healthy, you now look pale, so I am wondering if it is because we have talked about the fight and you got excited and lost so much blood? However, you look almost like a green calabash. I am sure nobody would say you are a coward as you have done such a great job, so you should calm down now. I have pliers in my bag for a smoking pipe and I have brought all I need to pull out an arrowhead. Be calm, I know a little of medical treatment. As I was given this set of armour by my master, I have a pair of gloves dyed with persimmon tannin. In case I get injured, I think these gloves will serve as a blood sucking bag. Remember, wounds can happen any time, whether you like it or not. Luckily, I have not been wounded so far.

草履取

Zoritori

The 'Sandal Carrying' Servant[37]

By

Kasuke

I have carried this musket in a long umbrella bag all the way here to this battlefield. Once the battle begins, I am going to hand it over to my master to shoot. My master told me to wear it around my waist if the

---

37   Of slightly higher status than the 'shoe box' carrying servant. This person would place the sandals of the samurai on the floor for him to step into.

enemy get too close. Actually, he only used it when it was effective and when it was useless, he then gave it to me and took his spear instead. I have never heard of such a ridiculous thing! I wear it on my waist like a sword, but cannot draw it to kill the enemy as it is not a sword but is a musket. Because of this, I thought it was so bad that I was told to carry such a useless thing, even more useless than a stick, but it turned out that I successfully smashed open an enemy's head thanks to this weapon! Here is my tale.

This is what happened. First, both ourselves and the enemy found each other and a shootout began, and bullets came over us like beans scattered in the Setsubun bean-throwing ritual. Then the arrow fighting began too. Now we had arrows and bullets all together; it was as if you had thrown a mass of chopsticks at all once, however, we were fine, even with this danger. After this noisy mess – which was like throwing a Kokirikodake[38] instrument and juggling balls all at once – we got close to the enemy. My master told me to put the musket on my waist and that he should be the first one to make a dash at the enemy with a spear. Then I told him I would back him up by shooting the musket, as he was fighting with a spear, and that he should give me enough gunpowder for at least one shot. At this request he became very angry and roundly scolded me, saying I was so audacious and way out of line in thinking I could back him up while spear fighting. So I had nothing to do but just relax and watch my master fight.

He fought a good spear fight with the first enemy soldier and killed him, then cut off his head. I wondered if I should help him, but I thought that he, as such a great fighter, could defeat ten or even twenty of the enemy. Therefore, I pretended not to notice his feats but in my mind I was thinking I should hit someone with the musket, if such a chance should arise. So, I crouched on the floor with my eyes closed as if taking a nap. Then I saw a man who had a melon-head[39] nearing my lord with a sword in hand, so I hit him with a good strike to the head, carefully aimed with this gun. Luckily, it hit him right on the head and the musket-sight lodged firmly in his skull and this melon-headed man kicked the bucket in an instant. I took that fruit-like head for myself, like a ripe fruit from a tree.

38   A percussion musical instrument made of strung bamboo slats. usually played with a 'clapping' and waving motion.

39   The text actually states 'persimmon' but 'melon-head' has the correct connotations in English.

At this my master said; 'Remember, taking just a nose in battle is banned, this is because people cannot identify the man and people may think you killed your own ally, however as lots of allies just saw you do this deed, you may just take the nose alone.' Before getting this head, I was wavering a lot but once I got the head, I began to feel delighted. I knew it would be too heavy if I tried to take the head with me, and as just the nose was less weight, it would be easy to collect more, even bad looking heads, probably enough to fill five or even ten horse loads. So I cut off just the nose as proof of my deeds. In this situation, people normally keep a nose under their breastplate, but as I'm not wearing armour I had to think about where to put it, if I put it under my kimono I was afraid I might lose the precious nose, so I considered this and finally decided to put it into the bottom of the musket bag and put the musket on top of it. However, just as I was doing this, I had a sudden stomach-ache because of my tape-worms and crumpled over; then a bullet hit my body and went through it! I was glad it went through[40] but then I hit the ground, landing on my arse. I wonder if I got this karma from me smashing the melon-headed man, but just then – after this bullet – I had an arrow pierce my head on one side. In haste I tried to remove it instantly but the shaft came out and the arrow head became stuck and would not come out. Everyone there was laughing at me and saying I looked like Ikkakusennin[41] with his horn!

My master gained two great achievements in the battle and I wanted to show how well I had done and took out the nose from the musket bag, but what I was told was this: when you cut off the nose, you should cut off the lips with it as well. If you only cut off the nose and it does not have a moustache (or stubble) you cannot tell if it is from a man or woman. So it cannot be proof of you having taken a man's head. My master told me off, saying this while goggling his eyes like a crab! This means that having that nose was useless and so I threw it away, my credit and achievement vanished with it. Thus, with effort, I had to give up the prestige of taking the head, what a shame! If I had not been injured, I would have picked up twenty packs or so of heads! Then I would ask for this musket to be given to me as a reward and I would have offered it to the gods to pray for the heads I would have taken. This is a matter of great regret!

---

40   Literally 'it was good' most likely he is happy that the bullet did not lodge inside his
        body.
41   A legendary ascetic with magical powers and a horn on his forehead.

Also, I cannot see my master's spear holder anywhere. He gave the musket back to me and took the spear but the holder has gone and I cannot see him anywhere. Now that the battle has ended he should reappear soon.

Look! I am now not classed as a coward but please pull the arrow out of my head carefully! If you try to pull it out roughly, there shall be lots of blood[42] and pain. Secure my head to a tree then pull it out. Remember do not pull out an arrowhead with your hands. You should use pliers or pincers if they are available. (Fig 11)

夫丸
Bumaru
Labourer
By
Yasuke

Sasuke-dono, Sasuke-dono, you have performed a great feat! Calm down, sit and relax now. I will take off your tannin[43] clothes and put my gown on you instead. As I have got no Haori jacket, I have been wearing a Nunoko quilted coat with its hem tied up and tucked under the sash so it looks like a Haori jacket. As you are only chugen, a servant, it is no surprise you might not know you should not wear something dyed with persimmon tannin. Even the great samurai people have brought tannin dyed clothes such as Tenugui cloths or arm or leg wear.[44] The arm and leg wear that Sasuke is wearing is dyed with persimmon and tannin, but you, Sasuke-dono, have white cloth as a Tasuki band around your shoulders. Why are you wearing that?

Sasuke replies: I cut white cloth to the length of a fathom[45] and made a Tasuki cloth so that if my master gets injured, I can secure him on my back with this cloth.

---

42 There is a slight play on words here which connotes becoming dizzy, for comic effect.

43 Tannin is mentioned here with a warning, as any wound with clothes dyed with tannin near it will bleed more.

44 Literally 'arm and leg bags' probably leggings and gauntlets.

45 6ft in the imperial system.

Well, well, it is really admirable for you to know the ancient ways that well. It is very sensible of you to do the above. I have heard of some bow or musket ashigaru and spear carrying servants that have a white sash on their armour for that very purpose. In case anyone gets injured, they will take off the sash on the armour and hold the injured one on their back by securing them with it. They can also untie the Tenugui cloth they have put around their head and use it as a sash instead. In case you do not use a Tenugui cloth as a sash, you should use the string of your quiver, bullet satchel, or your ration bag to tie around your body, above your armour, so that you can get your breastplate secured and move more easily. I am afraid I am about to make an uninvited remark, however I will continue. I think there are two different ways to retrieve an injured person from a battle, dependent on the time and opportunity. When the enemy is close and you have a hail of bullets or arrows, you should carry the injured one on your breast, so that you can carry him while protecting him with your body against enemy arrows or bullets. Even if an arrow or a bullet hits you, they will not hit the injured man. When you return with an injured person at a distance from the enemy it is difficult to carry him at your breast, so you may hold him on your back instead.

Also, Sasuke-dono, the string of your armoured skirts will snap early on, I think it is because the string was dyed black. Many people prefer black attachments for their armour as it looks great, but some people say that black dyed material, apart from lacquer ware, should not be used on armour.

Sasuke-dono, sit with your legs crossed firmly. I used to work for a surgeon carrying his medicine box, so I have learned a little about wounds by observing him. Do not bend right back or forward and do not lie down. Do not expose yourself to wind and do not talk in a loud voice, laugh or get angry and never fall asleep. If you fall asleep, I will stroke the tip of your nose with a paper string. You should not take hot or cold water, you should not even eat porridge. However, softly cooked rice will be fine. If the wound hurts too much, drink your own urine and it will relieve pain. Keep your urine in your battle hat or anything like this and cool it down. Then warm it later when you want to clean your wound with it, so that it will relieve the pain that the wound causes.

夫丸
Bumaru
Labourer
By
Mosuke

I am starving; this is because we had to run about hard all this morning. So I say, let us cook some food! Hey, you undo one bead from your ration bag that you have around your neck and put it in here. Put it as it is, I mean in the cloth bag. If it is only a two- or three-day battle, we can do without eating anything. However, if it is a five- to seven-day battle, then eating uncooked rice will also do. However, when in battle we don't know how long it will take. Also, all ashigaru and servants have a 'pan' on their heads,[46] so remember that we have to cook rice until it is soft, so that it will not give us stomach trouble.

My master does not have a wooden lunch box because he was called for war in haste, and he could not get his box prepared at such short notice. So he took the bowl that he would usually use for meals by chopping off the foot-stand[47] and wrapping the bowl with a Tenugui cloth and put it on his horse. I will offer him the meal in this bowl.

Kasuke-dono, Kasuke-dono, even though you are injured and have become faint, remember not to drink water or hot water as usual. First you should calm yourself down. You have been talking too long about your own bravery, so much so that you are getting tense, so that a lot of blood is oozing from the injury on your body and you also bleed internally. If you boil the dung of a grey horse, mix it in water and drink it, then the blood will exit your body and the wound will soon get better. It is said that drinking the blood of a grey horse will also do to ease the blood spilt in your abdomen. However, horse blood is not always available whenever you want it to be, so it would be better to eat dung. Thinking of this, you should take a grey horse when you go to war.

---

46 This 'pan' refers to the foot soldier's helmet, it is a comical statement suggesting they should cook food in their headgear.

47 Rice bowls used to have small 'feet' on the bottom.

It is of no wonder to me that your blood is spurting from the wound, as I now see you are wearing a persimmon tannin dyed Hitoemono, which is a single layered kimono. Persimmon tannin dyeing used on your clothes makes you bleed more and is not good for sword or arrow wounds. Put on Yasuke's coat instead (as it is not dyed in this way).

After we finish eating the rice we are now cooking, we should boil the roots of the rice plants we dug up and got in enemy lands and feed the horses with those roots. But remember that we should not dig up rice fields in our allied territory as it would damage next year's harvest! However, when in the enemy territory, dig them up whenever you see them.

鎗蒙

Yari Katsugi
The Spear Carrying Servant
By
Koroku

When spear fighting in today's battle began, our allies overwhelmed the enemy and clashed hard and then gave chase. My master was on the front line and on the left flank, while I was on the right flank, taking a respite. However, I was pushed forward in the advance. I wanted to stay put but could not and managed to stop myself by clasping to a hackberry tree. At this point I had been pushed forward a distance of 5 or 6 cho and I am now crouching down here, in this spot. They probably thought I had fled but it has turned out that in fact I have advanced!

Shinroku says: Koroku, Koroku, why are you carrying that sword? It seems to be a sword for a samurai, one who is attending the lord's palanquin, that is those who wear a long Haori Jacket, so I ask you why are you carrying it?

Koroku says: Well, I tried to look [like a samurai], those who wear a long Haori Jacket[48] but I had a scabbard that was too long for my sword,

---

48   The word samurai is implied here, the text only says long Haori jacket, meaning he wished to wear one like a samurai.

this is because while fighting this morning, I was jostled and broke the tip of the scabbard so that the end of the blade is now sticking out. What a pity! Shinroku, what do you think I should do?

Shinroku says: Well Koroku there's a good way to get a new scabbard.[49] In today's battle, lots of people took the heads of those running away and from those people who were detached from their groups.[50] Each of the fallen have a sword upon them, take a scabbard from them and use it for your own sword.

Koroku says: Yes I will do that! I remember one samurai – from another troop – he was detached from his troop, like I am lost now, but in the end he found his own troop and tried to re-join them. However, he had only been wearing one identifying mark on his shoulder but it had been torn off save for only a little bit of the cloth. Also, he did not have the other two kinds of identifying marks and when asked to say the password, as he was flustered, he could not remember the code-word and each troop he came to shunned him and moved him on. In time they began saying that the enemy had mixed in with us, and he was beheaded in the end. If he had had marks all around on the head, fore-head, neck, backbone, or arse, or tail like me, he could have got back in his own troop safely with no trouble. But he only had one mark and it was torn off and he had no other marks to identify him. Unfortunately, he forgot the password as well and was therefore beheaded by his allies, quite unexpectedly for him. The law says you should not get mixed in with other troops and this is why. Also, throwing away your identifying marks or forgetting the password is a seriously stupid thing to do, and it is a grave violation of the laws. This makes me wish I could pierce my nose, my ears, my jaw and put rings there to fix these identifying marks in place, what do you think?

Shinroku says: No, no, even with these four or five identifying marks here and there upon me, I am worried that I might drop and lose them and thus they may be taken by the enemy. So I do not want to be responsible for any more than these that I have!

Koroku says: Yes I agree. Looking at the battlefield yesterday and today, I saw countless numbers of musket bags, saddle covers, blankets,

---

49 Here the author uses the word for a second wife to add humour.
50 This could either be the case that the troops who were separated from the main group were killed, or that in their flight they throw down their arms.

stirrups, horse ladle and so on that have their clan crests upon them. This is extremely dishonourable. These days it is popular to have a war-screen (board) that is covered in gold leaf with the lord's crest in black upon it or a war-curtain (cloth) with pictures drawn or also the crest on it. This way was not followed by samurai families in former days. If you have crests upon such things and if a fire breaks out, you just cannot leave them behind. The war curtains are light-weight so you can fold them and place them on your back. The folded screens will take at least four or five people to carry just one of the pair of them on their backs, and they have to go around among the crowd with it like a Yakaragane[51] performer. What's the point of this? Is it to save the gold leaf of that crest?[52]

Shinroku says: Well I have no idea of the answer. Instead of the crest, it is better to draw a kite, pig, turnip, Japanese radish, Japanese chest-nut, Japanese honey locust, or anything like this, so you can leave the screens behind in the case of fire. This way you can take a sack of rice or other such things instead of the crested items, and then when you return to the remains of the fire, you can enclose yourselves with the war-curtain and you can enjoy a rice meal beneath its protection.[53] Apart from Hata-flags or Umajirushi standards,[54] it is best not to put crests on such things as helmets or helmet-hats, armour, sashimono-standards, Kasajirushi hat identifying 'ribbons', Sodejirushi sleeve markings, stirrups, satchels that lower soldiers carry – this is because they may well be captured by the enemy and used. It is disrespectful to put the lord's crest onto those items that could be discarded and taken up by the enemy.

[Unknown speaker]:[55] I am saying this because, in the event of an unparalleled fire like that of Edo which took place on the eighteenth

---

51 A street performance in the medieval period. The performer, with a number of drums hung from the neck, beats and swings them while dancing.

52 This is heavy with sarcasm.

53 This appears to mean that when a soldier returns to an area that has been torched, he can pick up any war-curtains that are left and use them against the elements or heat of the ashes and take his meal.

54 These flags generally stay at the rear of an army and, therefore, it is acceptable to have crests on them.

55 This paragraph is not included in the printed version of 1846 but is found in transcriptions from the mid-Edo period.

and nineteenth days of the first month, and of Meiryaku 3 [1657], bits of burnt paper were blown so far from Edo that they were scattered as far as the coasts of Boshu. It even happened that a local peasant happened to see a bit of burnt paper and was frightened out of his wits to find it was an accounting book of an honourable Jito estate steward. Concluding that Edo was on fire he went to the capital to see if the Jito estate steward was ok and carried with him – on his horse – rice, soy beans, straw, bran, etc. Thinking of this story, you must understand, if a screen with the lord's crest is abandoned and left behind and is burnt and blown away by wind, people will create rumours that the screen was once used in the guard house of the lord, which would be a great shame.

並中間

Nami Chugen

The Middle Servant

By

Shinroku

Koroku, Koroku, what you said is quite right. We all have three or even four identifying marks so I believe none of us will suffer the fate of the man in your story who was beheaded before even fighting the enemy.

Now I will tell you about when we beat and crushed the enemy. First it began with a fight with muskets between the vanguards of both sides. Then it was followed by arrow launching and Banaka-no-Shobu duels.[56] To be Ichibanyari or first spear, you have to be the person who won the first spear fight and it is regarded as the greatest achievement in battle, and is then followed by Nibanyari the second spear, who is the second person to win a spear fight. Then came those who have achieved the Yarishita,[57] which is to kill an opponent with a spear and Kuzushigiwa[58] that is those who kill by taking advantage of the gaps

---

56 Spear fights and duels to be performed by brave warriors in the middle of the two sides before the two sides get to close in on each other.
57 To take a head with a spear.
58 After Ichibanyari and Nibanyari have occurred, this is to kill an opponent by exploiting the breaking up of the enemy lines as the fighting starts.

created in the enemy. All these were locked in a fierce struggle, grappling[59] and stabbing and so heads were cut off or plucked, what a great clash it was today! Some people – to cover up the fact that they may have killed their own allies – collect as many heads as possible and cut off only the nose, one after another, and some thread these noses and wear them around the neck like prayer beads, as they have too many to put under their breast plate!

While those who were all fighting on fiercely, thinking it was their last moments to either die or achieve, thirty of the [mounted] samurai from eastern provinces joined the fierce battle at the correct place and with the correct timing. Then, before the second troop could begin to advance and fight, the flank attack [of our side] was halted and the thirty mounted warriors charged the enemy, some carrying spears, others a sword, a bow or a musket.

As the thirty warriors attacked from the enemy's right, thus the enemy could not make any thrusts or shots. If they had attacked from their left[60] side they could have given a counter with at least some thrust or fought back; but as they had the cavalry coming from the right they just fell into confusion and panic.

As soon as the mounted warriors attacked from the right, the rest of the vanguard began shooting muskets from the flank and they did not have any way to defend against it and their formation collapsed completely. In today's warfare everyone gets off their horse when fighting and fighting on horseback has been out of use for a long time, so the samurai from the Kamigata western provinces are different from those from Kanto eastern provinces and are not so well trained in horse riding, meaning that they were not well prepared to defend against these ways, this is my guess anyway.

Koroku: Shinroku, Shinroku, do not defame the Kamigata people so much! As we all saw, while passing the coast yesterday, a ship of seventy or eighty oars, though we don't know where it is from, was trying to fight against a middle-sized boat that was getting close to them, they were moving back and forth from the starboard to the larboard. They did not have enough ballast and they had too many people on board and had miscalculated the capacity.

---

59 Kunzu kumaretsu, literally, 'grapple while grappling' or 'to wrestle'.
60 It is easier to defend against an enemy attacking from the left.

The ship keeled over and did not recover so everybody ended up dying a dog's death. They were those samurai from the eastern provinces and did not know much about how to sail, so they all died for nothing. If it were the western samurai, they would balance the ship by dividing the troops into groups on both sides, so while those on one side were taking a nap, those on the other side would fight in defence, thus keeping the boat in balance. So those from the east, while knowing well how to ride a horse, do not know how to sail a boat, it is like an angler fish climbing up a tree. That is why I say you should not slander the Kamigata people so much. (See Fig 12)

又馬取
Umatori
The Groom
By
Magohachi

As it seems we won in today's battle, I guess we are going to have to cross the river for sure. The river will rise because it rained yesterday and the current will be even faster than an arrow. So I have twisted the reins hard, tightened the girth firmly and tied the stirrups up with a rope. I was thinking of removing and throwing away the saddle skirt, instead you should put it onto the rear saddle rings like a cover on the horse's arse. I did this because I can use this as a mat for my master as he has none. When going in the enemy lands, as it is a time when the wheat has an ear [and is ripe], we can cut it and collect it in a metal helmet, then we rub the wheat with the back side of the skirt between where it is folded over, we do this so the spikes will be gone. So, this skirt is useful and I have put it on the rear saddle rings, which I think is a very good idea.

又馬取
The Groom
By
Hikohachi

Magohachi, you did a good job. However, before, I brought up a point at the riverside, did you hear what I said? (See Fig 13)

Magohachi says: As there was too much noise, that of shooting muskets, I was almost deaf so I could not hear anything. Tell me what happened.

Hikohachi says: We two grooms can swim a little bit so we should grab both sides of the horse's bit and make the horse swim by pulling it into the water. If we are tired, we will be able to use the horse's bit as an aid which will help us swim with ease. When you ride the horse into the river, it will always try to rear up on its hind legs. To deal with this, the sandal carrying servant can swim a little – well, by swim I mean at least swim in the depth of a trench, you should have him hold onto the horse's tail, so if the horse tries to rear up, he will lift the tail up (which forces it down) and, therefore, it will make it swim. If you do it like this, the horse will swim as flat as a large wooden chest when it floats in water. The two Wakato retainers and the spear carrying servant do not float on water, [some people sink] like a bullet sinks, so, we should make them grab the ends of the straps of the crupper – after shortening the straps of course.[61]

I said to the master that if these five people hold onto the horse like this, there will be no way we cannot cross a river, no matter how big the river is and no matter how fast-flowing it is. However, the master did not answer nor say a word but smiled like a Pindola god and nodded a few times as if he was choking on pepper. By this I took it that he liked my idea, and so he rode the horse into the river with a loud splash. This horse – the one he has now – is as good as the one which was called Ikezuki[62] and was owned by the lord of Kamakura and he was the first horse in the Battle of Ujigawa, as the rider of this horse only had to hold the reins until it crossed over without difficulty. However, other horses barely managed to reach the other side, being swept away by the fast flow and moving in an arc.

---

61 This means a six-man team may cross: two holding the bit, two holding the rear of the saddle, one holding the tail and the samurai riding it.

62 Minamoto-no-Yoritomo, the founder of Kamakura shogunage.

As our master rode straight to the other side, all six of us together, our master and we followers, were the first ones to reach the opposite bank. Scarcely had the saddle got above water when the master got himself ready on horseback and with this he soon rode onto the other side and successfully got the head of an enemy, which was very impressive indeed. Anyway, it is most important for us two to agree on these points beforehand.

When there is a battle on foot and we have undermined the enemy and begin to chase after them as they flee, it surely is not easy for our master to mount immediately and give chase. Lots of battle standards are the same in the same clan so there is something called a Dashi on the top of the standard [a mark to differentiate each person]. Our master's one is the in the shape of a Sakabayashi[63] which is a ball of cedar leaves. We should keep sight of it and get the horse to him as soon as it is needed. We really have to remember this. Generally, battle standards, even if they stand out, are good if they have an easy name to call out. This is because when things get busy, [lower people] do not call out a person's name but the name of the standard or Dashi they use. So, it should be something common, but things such as misokoshi,[64] setsukai,[65] surikogi,[66] kaishakushi[67] etc., are so long to say and not so easy to call out. So any kind of marks, including battle-standards or war-curtains [as these two things are called by the design that they have upon them] should have images that are known to people, servants or labourers alike, and they should be short words.

When crossing over a river, some horses take in too much water. For those horses, mix lime and water into a solidified substance and put it into the arse, this will make them pass the water quickly. After that, feed them, but not much; little by little.

Magohachi says: Hikohachi, Hikohachi, that is a 6-year-old[68] horse and in its prime! On the second day after we left Edo, when we crossed

---

63 A ball made of cedar leaves and used as an offering to the god of wine.
64 A kitchen tool, miso strainer.
65 A kitchen spatula.
66 A wooden pestle.
67 A shell ladle.
68 In Japan they named the horse as a 1-year-old on the day of its birth, thus the horse here is actually 5 years old.

the Sako River in Soshu,[69] having had heavy rain for two days in a row, the river was so high that the horse was soaked up to its trunk, and it had a very flustered look about it. This is fair enough, as this horse was sold by some Hatamoto, and has had its four leg tendons sliced (which is a modern trend). Because of this, I thought it would not be easy for the horse to cross the river, so I kept holding the neck to support him. As I expected, it was struggling and twisting its body in the water, and the horse ended up collapsing as it was a Yadauma blunted horse. Our master ended up nearly drowning, as the river was so rapid and we humans and horse were almost carried out to sea, bringing us close to death. However, our master is a good swimmer and has acquired experience from travelling to Edo and accompanying the lord every other year and he saw that the river was very high and took off some of his clothes, that is his Haori jacket, Tattuke pantaloons and lower 'leggings' and then he tucked his kimono up, which allowed for his narrow escape. Actually, we all barely escaped death.

Now I feel so annoyed, thinking it happened all because this horse is a Yadauma horse with its tendons sliced. The Sako river is not even that big but you cannot say it is safe at any time! Whether the river is high or not, you cannot feel safe or at ease if you have to handle such a horse as this. This is even more so when you cross over a big river, like the River Oi. In fact you should pull the horses head with a rope and pull it along.

Hikohachi says: Magohachi, Magohachi, what's your opinion? It is said that horses are as essential for samurai as their feet, but if so I wonder why they do such things to horses? Some samurai cut the tendons of such precious horses and make them all useless. It is much better to lift the horse's tail and put Japanese pepper seeds into its arsehole.[70] This seems to be done to show people their horse and win praises. Today's samurai are so stupid, as they do what a horse dealer does and make their well bred horses totally useless!

Magohachi says: Hikohachi, what did you say? What a strange thing to do! I have some more strange things to tell you, so listen carefully. If a horse gets thinner, they try to fatten and feed it three-year-old vintage sake, to help nourish it. In summer, keep the horse within a mosquito

---

69   Present Kanagawa prefecture.
70   They give no reason for this.

net so that it will not be bitten by mosquitoes. Or when riding them in a riding ground, put straw mats all the way round the stable floor so that their hooves will not get muddy. As all the feed is carefully chosen, it must be of taste good. However, the horses of today must be really annoyed, as they have been made useless and weak by this practice of slicing the tendons.

Hikohachi, just try to look at it from the horse's point of view, even if the feed is not so good, they would prefer not to have their tendons cut I guess. What do you think?

Hikohachi says: That sounds quite right Magohachi-dono. What a shame it is! Even such humble grooms like you and I think lame-legged horses will not do any good, but how could today's samurai favour such lame-legged horses, it is really strange.

Remember, you should be prepared, as the River Oi is just at the foot of the Hakone Mountain range and the river is always rapid, so much so that even a stone as big as a Nagamochi long chest may be carried away. Think of the horse that collapsed in the Sako River as in the story above, imagine if that horse collapsed in the River Oi, together with our master, we would all be swept away all at once, maybe as far as Iro'o town, which is far away. Keep this in mind and be prepared!

Magohachi says: Oh how annoying it is. These things have been brought about only because we have purchased such a horse. What do you think Hikohachi-dono? Life is most precious, so to avoid these things I want to serve a clan which does not like such weak horses next year. What say you?

Hikohachi says: Magohachi, Magohachi, you are quite right. Life must be the first consideration. I will do the same thing as you next year.

Related to this, I have just remembered a small trinket of information. My father once told me a story and it is still ringing in my ears. Now I will tell it to you, so you listen now, with your ears open wide:

A long time ago, Lord Kusunoki led his army of 10,000 people and left Kyoto at the time between the hours Tiger and Hare [about 5 a.m.], and journeyed the equivalent of two days travel in one day and reached as far as Onohara, which is east of Mikusayama on the border between the three provinces of Tanba, Settsu and Harima, he arrived there as early as the hour of Dog (around 7-9 p.m.) of the next day. My father heard a blind monk in Hayamonogatari storytelling and he told me his story, and I have kept this story with me for seven or eight years or so. In those days they rode horses so well, just like this, but these days the samurai strangely like to have this new craze of lame legged horses. Magohachi, what do you think of this?

Magohachi says: Hikohachi, everything you say is quite right. While listening to you, I too have remembered one thing. I will tell you now, so please listen. I heard that Lord Kusunoki liked those horses that were good at galloping and not so easy to tire, even after a long journey, is it true or not? Well, this is what I heard from the monk of our family temple, so what do you think?

Hikohachi says: Magohachi, Magohachi, this is very interesting indeed. For that reason, today's samurai try to imitate the way of a horse trader, but they should choose strongly built horses, those horses that people no longer give praise to any more. As horse traders deceive people to sell their horses for as much money as possible, it seems that only money matters to them. Today's samurai behave like horse traders in this way, so that they try to cheat people; but what they do not know is, they will be tricked by people in the end. What a stupid thing to do! Just to show off a delicate horse to people they follow this custom! Rather than having Yamabushi or monks pray for success in war, it would be much better if they did not have their horse's legs blunted in this fashion – then they would have no need for prayers. Among all the hundreds of horses, more than half the number are Yadauma lame-legged ones, so they are not very useful. This is because the reign in this land has been so peaceful and those who fought in the Battle of Sekigahara or the Sieges of Osaka have all died, and even those in the Battle of Shimabara are now so old that they are bent like shrimp and turning senile, so that they cannot give an opinion on the matter. The samurai of today know nothing!

Look at what will happen with such a horse. You do not have to wait for times of war to see the result of these poor horses. For example at the event of the Shogun 'going up'[71] to Kyoto, and if our master needs to accompany his Lordship, in the Doyo season of the sixth month,[72] then almost all the Yadauma style horses will drop dead by the time they

---

71 They traditionally used the word 'up' when visiting Kyoto as the Emperor is in residence.

72 The first month is in February and, therefore, this is July/August when it is extremely hot.

pass through Hakone. Only after the samurai are choked by the smell of rotten horses, dead on Hakone Pass, will they realise the reason for this and learn this lesson well.

Musha Monogatari, Tales of the Samurai, 1654

VOLUME ONE

Article 1

According to an old samurai story, Ota Dokan Nyudo Mochisuke, from Edo of Bushu, when he went up to Kyoto for the first time, met the emperor who said to him, 'as you live around Sumida river in Edo, you must know much of hooded gulls'.[1] To this, Dokan replied with the poem:

年ふれどまだしりざりし都鳥隅田河原に宿はあれ共
Despite those many years I have lived there, I have not known
Miyakodori, though I have lived on the riverside of Sumida

The emperor was impressed with this poem and composed a poem in reply:

武蔵野はかやはらの野と聞しかどかゝることばの花も有哉
Though I heard that Musashino is a field of plume grass, I was impressed
that there are such beautiful flowering words too

Article 2

According to an old samurai story, Genzanmi Nyudo Yorimasa killed himself at Byodoin of Uji, at which point he said to his men, 'Do not bury my bones in Byodoin, put them in a pilgrim's bag and perform ascetic practices around various provinces with the container hanging from your neck. At one point you will see an auspicious sign at the place I would like to stay, bury my bones there.' At which point, he killed himself.

Following his last words, the men went from province to province as instructed. One of them, arriving in Koga in Shinousa province, rested and took the remains from around his neck and placed them on the ground. After a while he stood up and tried to take up the container with the intent of carrying on, however he could not lift it, which made him

---

1   The Japanese name for hooded gulls is Miyakodori, which literally means 'birds of the metropolis (Kyoto)', the concept was often used in poems at the time and is a play on words and this article is a subtle play between the two meanings.

wonder and think that maybe he should bury the bones there. Thus, he talked to the local people and buried the bones somewhere near Koga village. The traveller himself lived in a house near to the place of burial, leading a stoic and simple life until he died. To this day, Yorimasazuka, or the grave of Yorimasa, can be found in this place, which is now within Koga Castle. The area of the grave is now called Yorimasa's enclosure.

Article 3

According to an old samurai story, there is an auspicious small flag which has been used traditionally since Lord Tokugawa Ieyasu was young. It is a white cloth with a sutra written in black ink and it says:

厭離穢土欣求浄土

Getting weary and parting from this filthy world; and truly wishing to
go to heaven

The sutra was handwritten by a monk of the Jodo branch, whose name was Saint Osho Toyo of Daijuji temple of Mikawa province.

Article 4

According to an old samurai story, there were two strong samurai whose names were Kawada Yasuke and Narasaki Jubei, who served Kobayakawa Saemon-no-suke Takakage, who was the third son of Lord Mouri Uma-no-kami Motonari, the ruler of Chugoku.

At the time of the Siege of Odawara, Kawada, the first samurai – with a huge flag – and the other samurai, Narasaki, with an arrow-cape the size of 18 tan,[2] were walking from town to town on their way to battle. Lord Taiko Hideyoshi, who was then staying in Numazu of Izu province, saw them passing by with their huge flag and cape. The lord said, 'Look, what strong warriors they are! Go and ask them for their names.' At which point his mounted samurai immediately went and said to them, from horseback, 'Listen to this humbly, for this is from Lord Hideyoshi. The lord has said, "What a spectacular cape and flag you have! Go and ask them who they are." Therefore, could I have your names?' However, on

2   Tan – a unit for a roll of kimono cloth of about 11m.

hearing this they did not answer and the mounted messenger came back having failed. Hearing this from him, Lord Hideyoshi said, 'Maybe you asked them without dismounting from your horse, is this so? As that is a very rude thing to do, as those carrying such a huge flag or cape cannot be mounted, as no horse could bear them, no matter what rank of warriors they are, remember that they have to be on foot when they carry such things. If it is the case, why should they give their names over if you have questioned them from horseback?' He then ordered another man to ask them this time, not from horseback and because of this they replied.

Article 5
According to an old samurai story, Lord Akechi Hyuga-no-kami, when he was a low-ranking retainer, once happened to cross the Togo river of Echizen province and found a statue of Daikoku.[3] He was delighted and thought to himself, 'It is the god of good luck', and brought it back to his quarters and placed it in the corner on a shelf and worshipped it every morning and night with respect.

Someone heard of this and said to him, 'You have such a lucky god! This god is a ruler of 1,000 people. Keep your faith in him.'

With this, Akechi was very much surprised and said, 'I did not know this god governed only 1,000 people. What a narrow-minded god Lord Daikoku is! You do not have to be a god of luck to command that many people, there are so many ordinary people who also govern 1,000 men. Therefore, he is not a god that samurai should worship,' and so he threw it away.

Article 6
According to an old samurai story, it is always true that unfaithful samurai and thankless children are dishonourable, so much so that even those people of succeeding generations will hear their names and scorn them throughout time. Be careful, be careful. An old saying says:

---

3   The god of wealth.

Fig 1. Asahi Idezaemon is on the right. Yuhi Irizaemon is on the left. (See p. 16)

Fig 2. Ogawa Asaemon and Okawa Fukazaemon. (See p. 18)

Fig 3. Nagara Genzaemon is on the right. Kichinaizaemon is in the middle.
Sukenaizaemon is on the left. (See p. 23)

Fig 4. The Commander's Standard Bearer, Magozo is on the right. The Commander's Standard
Carrying Servant, Hikozo is on the left. (See p. 24)

Fig 5. The Musket Carrying Servant, Tsutsuhei is on the right. The Musket Carrying Servant, Teppei is on the left. (See p. 24)

Fig 6. The Bow Carrying Servant, Yazaemon. (See p.25)

Fig 7. The Box Carrying Servant, Yarokubei, is above. The Sandal Carrying Servant, Kirokubei, is below. (See p. 29)

Fig 8. The Groom Kinroku, is on the right. (See p. 33)

Fig 9. The Arrow Box Carrying Servant, Yazo is on the right. The Bullet Box Carrying Servant, Zundon is on the left. (See p. 38)

Fig 10. Yagi Gozo, the Quarter Master, is on the right. Bazo, the Labourer, is on the left. (See p. 42)

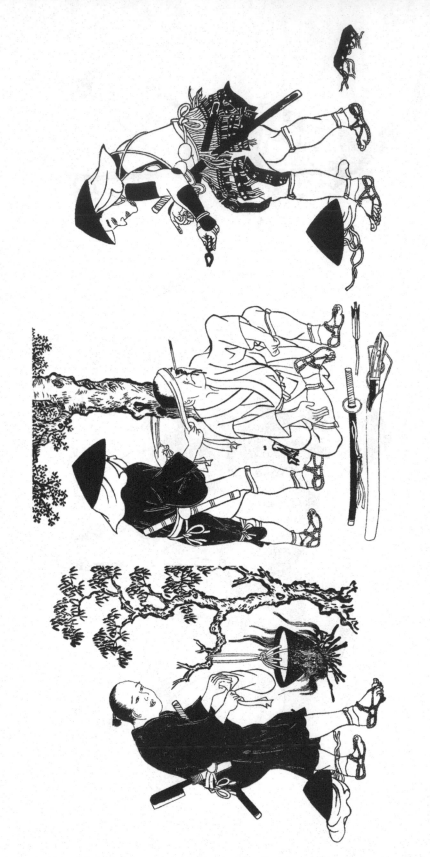

Fig 11. From right to left: Sasuke, the Young Lower Retainer. Kasuke, the Sandal Carrying servant. Yasuke, the Labourer. Mosuke, the Labourer. (See p. 46)

Fig 12. Koroku, the Lord's Spear Servant, is on the right. Shinroku, the Middle Servant, is on the left. (See p. 54)

Fig 13. Magohachi and Hikohachi. (See p. 55)

Fig 14. The flag of Jiki Hachiman. (See p. 71)

Fig 15. Samurai armour, which has rules pertaining to what colour thread can be used. (See p. 86)

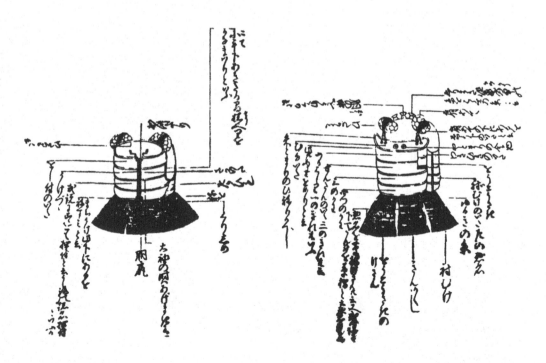

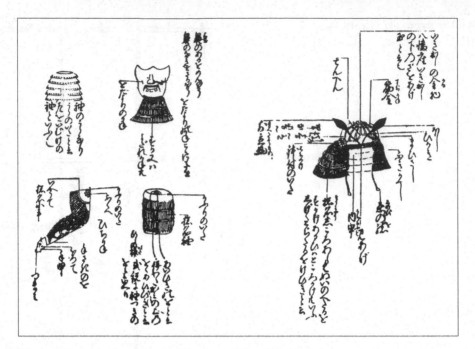

Fig 16. Information on armour and coloured thread. (See p. 86)

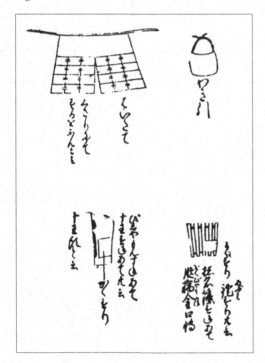

Fig 17. More information on armour and coloured thread. (See p. 86)

Fig 18. The five types of decapitated head. (See p. 95)

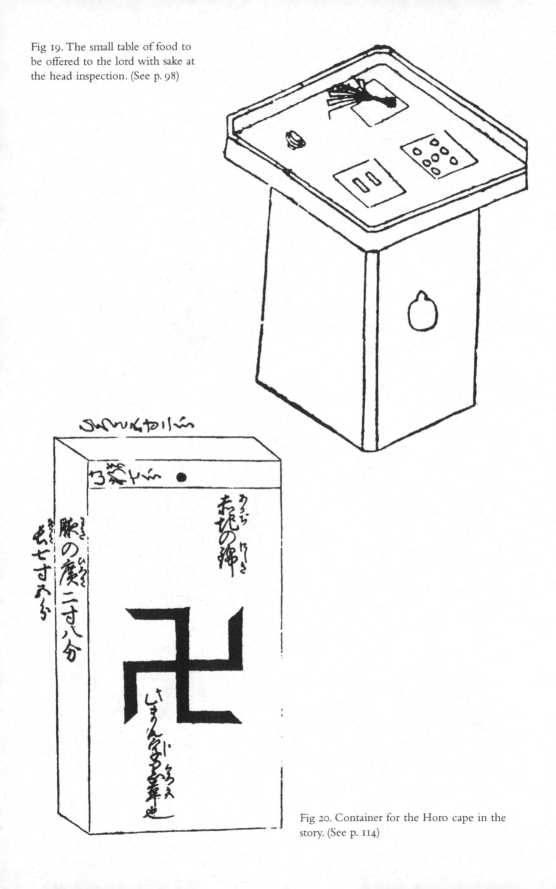

Fig 19. The small table of food to be offered to the lord with sake at the head inspection. (See p. 98)

Fig 20. Container for the Horo cape in the story. (See p. 114)

Fig 21. In the old nun's story, the teeth of the severed heads were blackened to show the best warriors: 'Remember, heads are not what you should be afraid of, back then we even slept among the heads with the smell of blood in the air.' (See p. 120)

Fig 22. The old nun, crossing a moat in a wooden washtub. (See p. 121)

Fig 23. The old nun's mother is carried by her father after delivering a baby girl. The baby has been bathed in the water of a rice field and is wrapped in the retainer's kimono. (See p. 121)

Fig 24. Kiku's escape from Osaka Castle. (See p. 124)

Fig 25. Lord Hideyoshi in the Yamazato tea rooms of Osaka Castle. (See p. 126)

忠臣必出孝子門
Faithful retainers always come from those whose family are made up of thankful children

Also, other old poems say:

幾度も主の命に替るべしふた心こそながき恥なれ

You should risk your life for your lord's life no matter how many times it is and disloyalty should be a disgrace longer than anything else

君をあふぎ親を思ひて仮初もたかき賤礼義みだすな

Look up to your lord and think much of your parents, so that you should always keep to the morals of order, high or humble

Article 7

According to an old samurai story, there were twelve direct orderlies within Lord Takeda Shingen's army. Each of them was supposed to carry a square flag of white cloth with a black centipede upon it. However, one of them, Hajikano Den'emon, was out with a white square flag without a centipede. Lord Shingen, seeing this, asked who was that of the twelve messengers that had only a white flag [and no insignia]. A reply said that it was Hajikano Den'emon. The lord became angry and asked him why he did not obey this rule. Den'emon said, 'I would never break the rules. I have a three-centimetre centipede just next to a side loop of the flag.' At which point he showed it to the lord. The lord asked him why it was thus. Den'emon said, 'If I had a centipede as everyone else has, whatever I do will be hardly distinguishable among others on the battlefield.' Lord Shingen laughed to hear this.

Article 8

According to an old samurai story, there was a brave samurai, whose name was Ogasawara Kento[4] and Niwa Gorozaemon-no-jo Nagashige was his master, who was the lord of Komatsu Castle in Kaga domain.

---

4   The ideogram for Kento means 'dog's head', which one must know to understand the story.

Kento was brisk and competent but clumsy and unsociable. For that reason his master Gorozaemon did not give him a very high stipend and Kento stayed in rather a low position.

There was a ronin, or mercenary samurai, whose name was Eguchi Saburozaemon. The master of the castle, Gorozaemon-no-jo, employed this man for quite a high stipend because he was well presented and conducted himself with honour. Hearing this, Kento the clumsy said to himself, 'Well, well, there is no one in Japan who does not know of Kento from Gorozaemon's clan, I am well known, but how could anyone think this newcomer's bravery could be good enough to serve this clan? Good grief, the wonder of it!' and waited impatiently for their meeting to come.

When the day came, Eguchi – the newly hired samurai – attended Komatsu Castle for the first time, and Kento was already there waiting for him. Once Eguchi appeared in the hall, Kento said to him, 'Is that you, who is the ghost of Eguchi-no-Kimi?'[5]

Eguchi said, 'Well, yes, I am. I wonder if it is you, that man I heard that has the head of dogs?[6] However, it is said that this dog's head[7] is actually a brave warrior, but that he is low in ranking as he is unsociable and of few words. It is not rare that a samurai is well disciplined if born in a samurai family, and so if you would behave in an impressive way, then you would be able to distinguish yourself even more as samurai. Though I have far less experience than you, I have worked as a mercenary here and there since I was young, and now I am well known. Some lords appreciate that and are willing to employ me for a very high stipend. If you stay with one clan and are as good as Fan Kuai of ancient China, know that you could be of a much higher ranking if you know about the ways of other domains. What a waste it is that you stay in the same clan and know nothing of others.' At this Kento was at a loss for words, and became very polite to Eguchi after that.

---

5   This refers to an old tale concerning the ghost of a harlot called Eguchi-no-Kimi.

6   As a quip, he uses the name Kento, which translates as 'head of a dog' to become an insult, he does this by changing the pronunciation of his name to Inu-no-Kashira.

7   This time he uses the correct pronunciation.

Article 9

According to an old samurai story, Mori Ranmaru,[8] an attendant of Lord Oda Nobunaga, once attended his lord by carrying his sword when he went to the toilet. While waiting for him, he counted the number of notches which were upon his scabbard.

The Lord knew that he had counted them and afterwards gathered his pages together and said, 'Try and guess how many notches there are on this scabbard. I will give this sword to the one who can guess right.' So everyone put forward their guess, all but Ranmaru. At which point Lord Nobunaga said, 'Ran, why do you not voice your guess?' To which he replied, 'Because I know the answer and have counted them.'

Lord Nobunaga was impressed with this answer and gave him the sword.

Article 10

According to an old samurai story, Honda Heihachiro Yasutoshi,[9] who was a retainer to Lord Tokugawa Ieyasu, became angry when he saw his sons practise with spears and said, 'Spear fighting on a battlefield is for rather low-ranking samurai. Those of a high rank should learn above all other things how to use the baton to command an army. When I was of low rank I fought with a spear, but later on I was promoted to this high rank, so I now do not need to fight with a spear and thus always think of how to command my army. You should be prepared, by learning how to deal with the baton and command our forces, to get ready for the time you need to take over from me. Therefore, do not learn the ways of low-ranking samurai.'

In my opinion:[10] In the Chu dynasty of ancient China, there was a master swordsman and a fellow retainer recommended him to King Xiang. However, the king said swordsmanship is only about fighting against one enemy, therefore he would rather learn how to kill millions of people and thus he never learned the art of the sword.

---

8 It is said that he and Oda Nobunaga had sexual relations with young men, this was known as Shudo, a common samurai practice.

9 Presumably a mistake, it should be Honda Heihachiro Tadakatsu.

10 This is the opinion of the unknown author.

Indeed, it seems inappropriate for the general to fight with a spear himself. Also it would be improper on a battlefield if the general does not know how to use the baton of command.

According to Genpei Seisuiki, at the Battle of Kotsubo, Wada Yoshimori tried to give the order for his army to withdraw, but they mistook it to mean attack the enemy and so they fought against Hatakeyama Shigetada. Yoshimori intended to convey to his retainers the following and this is what he said, 'Do not let my brother Yoshimochi be killed and with this I waved to them with an open hand at first, which my men mistook, so I wanted to call them back with something large and more distinct'. Then he had his men open forty or fifty umbrellas and waved them towards the troop, which again they mistook and so thought that they were being told to advance further and risked their lives fighting.

As a result they fought when they should not have fought because the general did not have the correct knowledge on how to use the baton of command.

Yet it seems unlikely that such a good general as Yoshimori did such a thing, so I wonder if it was not the author's mistake? This is still not clear to me.

Article 11

According to an old samurai story, there was a master bowman who used the strongest of bows, his name was Ibano Todayu and he was a retainer of Ikeda Musashi-no-kami Terunao. When hunting in the mountains of Bizen domain, an injured boar was dashing toward him and so he fixed a forked arrow to his bow and shot at the beast with enormous power. Obviously, [because of his skill] the arrow pierced the boar from the nose through to the tail and then hit a pine tree – of 5 sun in circumference – breaking the tree.

On another occasion, he bent the iron bow of Minister Yuriwaka, which was kept in the Sakaori shrine of Bicchu, he did this so strongly that it broke at the upper notch. Later he had it fixed and had words inlaid on the Hitaigi wooden plate which is on the upper part of a bow, it said, 'Ibano Todayu bent and broke this'.

Article 12

According to an old samurai story, Lord Ouchi Yoshitaka of the Suo province was called Sir Kamewaka-maru and when he was a child he once saw common children playing with money and said, 'I want to play with it too.' His attendant, Sugi Hoki-no-kami replied, 'Sir, that is too filthy and indecent a thing to be exposed to your view,' and then put a gold hairpin through the money and threw it away together with the hairpin in to the toilet, this was done to teach him.

Article 13

According to an old samurai story, the lord of Takatori Castle of the Washu province, Matsukura Ukon-no-dayu said, 'Warriors who are firmly determined will not be disgraced throughout their lifetime and will remain highly admired even long after death because of their resolution. On the other hand, weak and irresolute warriors tend to make mistakes more often than not, because of their lack of determination. A warrior, whose name was Yamamoto Matasuke, when walking on a path in the mountain, saw a yamakagashi[11] snake crawl out in front of him. He made such a fuss of it and jumped 3 shaku [90cm] to his side, where unfortunately he stepped on a venomous mamushi snake. At which point, he was bitten, being surprised and acting without thought he jumped back to where he was before to be bitten by the Yamakagashi snake too. He suffered long after that and became crippled in the end. This all happened because this man was not prepared and was so easily surprised or flustered.

A poem says:

なるこをばおのが羽風に任つゝ心とさはぐむら雀哉

Though the trinkets to scare the birds are clattering, moving because of the wind of the wings of the sparrows, the flock of sparrows themselves are thrown into confusion

A warrior should never be unprepared or surprised with such a thing, and consequently meet with disaster, this is completely shameful.

---

11 A tiger keelback, a venomous snake.

Article 14

According to an old samurai story, during the Summer Siege of Osaka Castle, Sanada Saemon-no-suke was killed by Nishio Nizaemon. This Nishio was a retainer of Lord Echizen Shosho Tadanao. Also, Mishuku Echizen-no-kami was killed by Nomoto Ukon, and this is the story of what happened.

Echizen-no-kami's original name was Mishuku Kanbei and he used to be a retainer of the original lord of Echizen [who was from the eastern forces], but for some reason he – Mishuku Kanbei – left Echizen and ended up staying in Osaka Castle.

He came to serve Lord Toyotomi Hideyori – who was in opposition – and requested to be given his home province of Echizen – so that he could control it – that is if the lord Toyotomi Hideyori won the war and conquered the country. So because of this he had named himself Echizen-no-kami – [which implies he was the lord of Echizen] making him a usurper. With this deal in place, he joined the troop of Sir Shosho. However, Mishuku Kanbei – the pretender – was attacked and almost defeated at the position where he was stationed, so Sanada Saemon-no-suke was sent to aid him, however the Echizen-troop, who were stationed at Osaka at the time, took advantage of the chance, attacked and killed them both.[12]

Article 15

According to an old samurai story, Hojo Saemon-dayu, who was a retainer of Lord Hojo Ujiyasu of Odawara in Soshu province, had a flag of tawny silk with just two ideograms written in ink upon it: 八幡. It meant, 'I am a direct follower of Hachiman Daibosatsu.' Therefore, it was called the flag of Jiki Hachiman.[13]

At the time of the assault on Fukasawa Castle of Soshu, this flag fell into the hands of Lord Takeda Shingen. He gave it to Sanada Genjiro

---

12 This story is complex due to the crossover of names and the insertion of names that do not actually have any relevance to the story. In short, a man was employed by the lord of Echizen, but as the lord dies he changes sides to join Toyotomi Hideyori in the hope that Hideyori would make him the next lord of Echizen, usurping his former lord's son.

13 Jiki has the double meaning of 'direct' and 'yellow cloth'.

Nobutada, who later succeeded the Katsuno family and changed his name to Katsuno Ichiemon. He was the youngest child of Sanada Ittokusai. I hear this said flag is still kept within the family.

6 shaku 9 sun [207cm] long.
3 shaku 6 sun [108cm] wide.
3 pieces of cloth wide.
It has six loops on the top, the side has a slot and there are details to be orally transmitted. (Fig 14)

Article 16
According to an old samurai story, there was a wandering samurai who was a very distinguished warrior in his military achievements and his name was Izutsu On'na-no-suke.[14] His outfits were like a female's and his hair was long and done in the style of Karawa, and he always wore a Hirabari needle in his hair, this was so people could not grab his topknot.

Article 17
According to an old samurai story, there was a samurai whose name was Tsukuda Mataemon.[15] He always used to relate the following story:

> If a lord says an unreasonable thing to his retainers, you should strictly refrain from countering it. The reason is when I was serving Gamo Ujisato of Aizu, at the time of a battle in the Oshu district, Ujisato went out to inspect the huts within the camp discreetly every night. One night we were subject to a night attack but we were able to fight back and defend ourselves successfully. On the next morning, we were called to review the previous night's battle. Ujisato said, 'As Tsukuda is always well-prepared, he was first to fight as expected. However, it seems he lost his head a little, you may not know but he thrust with his spear but without taking off the sheath.' To this, Tsukuda said, 'What you say is quite right, my Lord. It was a little cloudy in the evening, so I left with a rain cover on my spear. Since the night attack was so severe, I could not pull it off until the fighting had

14   The ideogram for on'na in On'na-no-suke means woman.
15   The composer of a set of famous war poems. First and third person are confused.

finished.' Ujisato was so impressed with his reply and said, 'Tsukuda is a very honest man. An ordinary man would not admit that he put a rain cover on his spear! He is a true Bushi.' And thus gave me a reward.

Even if it is cloudy, it would never be the case that I would take this spear out with a rain cover still on it, but I always want to agree with my lord and thus I spoke as I did.

Supplement: after Ujisato was transferred to a far and distant province, Tsukuda was employed by Fukushima Saemon-dayu, but ended up being burnt at the stake due to his belief in Christianity.

Article 18
According to an old samurai story, Ota Dokan Nyudo had a son who died before him and thus made these poems at the first anniversary of his death:

恨めしく又なつかしき月日哉別しこぞのけふと思へば
It is so regrettable and nostalgic at the same time while looking back to the old days, thinking of the farewell on the same day of one year ago

こぞのけふ別し時も今とても忘らればこそ思ひ出さめ
On the same day of last year, the time of our sad separation, I still can find no way to forget, I will bring it to mind again

Article 19
According to an old samurai story, a child of a samurai family should not be raised among merchants or peasants. It would be desirable to make him start learning reading and writing at the age of 8, and to be fully determined towards the martial arts at the age of 14 or 15. Even if the parents are poor and cannot provide for their children with an education or learning or the martial arts, they should at least raise their children among samurai. In the case where they are raised as common people, no matter how highborn they are, they will look and speak like humble people. Thus, in childhood they will say Gairu for Kaeru [frog] or Gani for Kani [crab]. Even after having grown up, they will speak as follows:

Sansho dono for Saisho dono (Prime Minister)

Ninbu dono for Minbu dono (name of an official rank)

Yuwami-no-kuni for Iwami-no-kuni (name of a province)

Jozoji for Zojoji (Name of a temple)

Kitsunegawa-no-gosho for Kitsuregawa-no-gosho (the palace at Kitsuregawa)

Kozaruhen for Kozatohen (the name of the left hand side of any Chinese ideogram)

Katsuubushi for Katsuobushi (dried bonito)

Taikeike for Taiheiki (name of a famous war chronicle)

Miyasu for meyasu (estimate)

Koyumi for koyomi (calendar)

Higuan for higan (the equinoctial week)

Sengyo for segyo (almsgiving)

Mutsuke for mokke (unexpectedness)

Shimotsu for shumotsu (boil)

Hakuran for kakuran (sunstroke)

Kakeuchi for kakeochi (elopement)

Injukiri for injikiri (making a hand gesture of In)

Ishigake for ishigaki (stone wall)

Ai for ayu (sweet-fish)

Shake for sake (salmon)

A poem on the subject of salmon:[16]

昨日たちけふきてみれば衣川すそのほころびさけ上るなり

I left yesterday and arrived here today to find the salmon going upstream

With the double meaning of:

Cutting out a kimono yesterday and trying it on today, it already has become unstitched at its hem

As well as the above, there are many other likely mistakes, these are only examples.

---

16   This poem has a double meaning and is an elocution lesson. It is a reference to the last word in the list given above, but is of course lost in translation.

Article 20

According to an old samurai story, this is a tale about the capturing of Ishida Jibunosho. He was captured alive in a bed of reeds in Wakizaka of the Asai district of Goshu province by Tanaka Denzaemon, who was a retainer of the lord of Okazaki Castle, whose name was Tanaka Hyobu-no-tayu. After being captured, Jibunosho took a Wakizashi short sword of 1 shaku, 3 sun [39cm] from the inside of his kimono and said, 'This was given to me by Lord Hideyoshi to remind me of him. It is a Kiriha Kanezane short sword.' Hyobudayu, on getting this Wakizashi sword, informed Lord Ieyasu of this. The lord gave him Chikugo province as reward, and this is how Hyobudayu became Tanaka Chikugo-no-kami.

Article 21

According to an old samurai story, I was shown some poems composed by ancient generals as follows:

Presented to Yakusiji Jirozaemon-jo Kinyoshi by Lord Ashikada Takauji

我家のかぜならなくに和歌の浦の波までかよふ道ぞ賢き
Even though it was not the way of his family, how smart it was for him to go that far on the path of poems

'Foggy Mountains' by Date Masamune:

山あいの霧はさながら海に似て浪かときけば松風のをと
Fog in the mountains appears to be similar to the sea, so I thought the sound was the sound of waves but I found it was the sound of the pine trees swaying in the wind

'Snowy Mountains' by Date Masamune:

中々につゞら折なる道絶て雪にとなりの近き山里
Trailing a winding snowy path in the mountain, I found it came to a dead end in the snow. Then it turned out that it was near a neighbouring village.

'Green Willow'[17] by Lord Mouri Motonari:

青柳の糸くり出すそのかみはたがをだまきのはじめなるらん
As the Odamaki[18] hemp yarn wound around a hollow ball that is spin-
ning out a thread, I wonder who on earth made the start of it all

'Quiet Retreat' by Lord Hojo Ujiyasu:

中々に清めぬ庭はちりもなし風にまかする峯のした庵
Even though the garden is not cleaned so often, it is absolutely spotless,
leaving it all to wind here in this hermitage at the foot of the mountain

'Cherry Blossoms Among Pine Trees' by Lord Takeda Harunobu

立ならぶかいこそなけれ桜花松に千とせの色はならはで
All cherry blossoms among pine trees are proven not to be
worthwhile,[19] thus being together as they are, [the Cherry Blossom] has
not learned to remain forever green

'An Ode of Celebration for the Pine Trees' by Lord Hojo Ujimasa

守れ猶君にひかれて住吉の松の千とせを万代のすゑ
May heaven keep our clan as the pine trees we see in Sumiyoshi now,
may it live for 1,000 years or even for 10,000

Title unknown, but composed by Lord Imagawa Ujizane:

中々に世をも人をも恨むまじ時にあはぬを身の科にして
I will not blame the world or people, accepting the blame of not meeting
the times as my responsibility[20]

---

17 'Green Willow' is often connected to thread or yarns.
18 A yarn spindle.
19 This is a play on words and has the same phonetic sound as Kai, Takeda Shingen's
domain.
20 This is a reference to his defeat in 1568 by Takeda Shingen.

Article 22

According to an old samurai story, Lord Nagao Kenshin had excellent generals, Naeo Yamashiro-no-kami, Kakizaki Izumi-no-kami and Amakasu Omi-no-kami, who were all well matched. The lord left Ecchu province in the care of Kakizaki.

One time Kakizaki put a horse of his own on sale in Kyoto. Lord Oda Nobunaga happened to know that the owner was Kakizaki and bought it at a high price and with haste. Also he sent a polite letter to Kakizaki, which said, 'This is a rare horse to have. If you have any other horses like this, I would be happy to buy them,' this was sent together with a kimono as a present.

Unfortunately, Kakizaki was so careless that he did not tell Lord Kenshin of this matter, so when Kenshin heard of this, he became very angry and killed him.

Later on, the ghost of Kakizaki appeared to Lord Kenshin, but the lord was so fearless and high spirited that he was not daunted by this at all.

However, the lord passed away soon after that, so people spread the rumour that the ghost of Kakizaki haunted and killed him.

Article 23

According to an old samurai story, at the event of the Battle of Ishigakibara of Bungo domain, there was a samurai whose name was Yoshihiro Kahei-no-jo who was the lord of Kakei Castle, and it must be said that he had sided with Otomo Shuri-dayu. One day he went scouting to understand the formation of his enemy, who were led by Kuroda Josui Nyudo Masanari. While scouting, Yoshihiro fought with Inoue Kurozaemon, who was a retainer of Masanari and was killed by him. The local people later built a stone monument for him at a beach called Beu, which was close to Ishigakibara, this stone was engraved with the name of Yoshihiro Kahei-no-jo.

As he was a famous samurai, right-minded samurai prayed when passing by it and the local people, if suffering from a high fever, conducted the purification rite of Shiogori[21] and offered rice and sake as they worshipped it. If this was done then they immediately recovered from the fever. The children of the dead samurai Kahyoe later heard of that stone

---

21 Bathing in sea water for purification.

and went to Beu and stood by the grave and said, 'As rice and sake are offered, this grave looks indecent. From now on, only the right Shiogori ritual will be performed and it will be enough to heal sickness, otherwise the fever will never lift.' Since that day, only by performing the purification rite of Shiogori would people be healed of their illness.

Article 24

According to an old samurai story, in Mikatagahara of Enshu province, at the battle between Lord Takeda Shingen and Lord Tokugawa Ieyasu, thousands of soldiers died by falling into a valley called Saigakake, which was between Mikatagahara and Hamamatsu. The spirits of the dead raised voices and rang out ear-piercingly to the fullest with their cry. Hearing of this, Lord Ieyasu asked help of a sage and the sage said he would appease the souls.

He performed the rite of Nenbutsuodori[22] from the thirteenth to the fifteenth of the seventh month of a lunar year, and made the correct constructions with silk. This festival was named Bindoro and they celebrated the dead for three days during the Bon period, which is the festival for the dead. With this, the voices of the dead stopped and the festival is still in practice to this day, or so I hear.

Article 25

According to an ancient samurai story, Matsuda Rokuro Saemon-no-jo Sadakatsu, who was a retainer of Lord Hojo Ujiyasu, said:

> Good Bushi with a number of great achievements do not talk about their feats all through their lives, no matter how many people ask them to. They do not talk but are renowned as incomparable, courageous and distinguished because they are extraordinary samurai.
>
> On the other hand, some Bushi who are not so good or who are good but in an ordinary way, that is those who get only two or three enemy's heads, have an avid desire for fame and talk about how great they are. If asked by people, they talk even more than ever, especially when talking to young samurai. It is like when you put sake in a barrel. When the barrel is

---

22   A way of Buddhist praying with chanting, drum beating and dancing.

filled with sake, it will not resonate very much, while it will sound very loudly with only a little sake.

Such braggarts are so clamorous because their feats are not very significant. I think that is a very reasonable thing to say. Also, I think this holds true with every kind of art. Those who pretend to have mastery of some art they have not mastered very well look so stupid to the eye of the observers.

A famous monk of Zen Buddhism, Takuan (1573-1645) composed the following poem:

麓なる一木の色を知がほに奥もまだみぬみよしのゝ花

Having seen only one cherry tree at the base of Yoshino mountain, you pretend to know all, but you do not know anything of the magnificent view of Yoshino when you are deep in the mountain and it is filled with cherry blossoms

The meaning of this poem seems very deep. Later on, Rokurozaemon went to serve the Shogun Hidetada as an Ohata Bugyo, that is a commander of the standards.

Article 26

According to an old samurai story, a samurai whose name was Konishi Manbei, and was 18 or 19 years old, came into the service of Sir Akechi Hyuga-no-kami with a high stipend and with the ambition to dedicate himself fully to this lord. Some samurai, on hearing this, questioned how such an immature samurai could do anything significant, for he would need nerves of steel. Others whispered that it was not very sensible for the lord to give him such a high stipend.

One time while Manbei was in the castle, some nosy young samurai came to him and said to Manbei, 'I do not remember exactly what your name is, is it Mabei or Manbei?' On hearing this, Manbei realised that he was making fun of him and replied, 'It depends on the level and fullness of your spirit. When you are highly spirited, you will call me Manbei with good pronunciation and when you are hungry or lacking in will, you can call me Mabei. It all depends on your spirit.' Then the disruptive samurai was embarrassed and retreated.

During the battle with Akai Akuemon, the lord of the Hotsuzu Castle of Tamba, Sir Akechi encamped within the area of Mt. Yahata. While he was observing his men he found a hut with Manbei and an older and newly recruited samurai sleeping deeply. The lord snuck in and took away their swords. The two samurai were so surprised when they awoke that the older samurai said, 'All this will be out when the day breaks. We should stab each other to death before dawn.' Upon this, Manbei contemplated for a while then said, 'There would be no benefit from us dying in vain. It would have been a deep disgrace if our swords were taken while awake, but it was while we were asleep and it should not be classed as our fault at all. If you really want to kill yourself, I must stress that I am not of the same opinion.' This meant that the older samurai could not commit suicide on his own.

However, when the day was nearly breaking, Manbei, wearing a red pennant, went over to the enemy camp and successfully put the pennant on the height within the enemy's encampment and was killed at length at the foot of the pennant. Both sides were amazed by his magnificent deed. It is rumoured that Sir Akechi's actions were a mistake.

Article 27

According to an old samurai story, Sue Owari-no-kami Takafusa, who was a chief retainer of Lord Ouchi Yoshitaka, plotted a rebellion against the lord and drove him into killing himself at Daineiji temple of Nagato domain in 1551.

The lord composed a death poem saying:

討人もうたるゝ人ももろともに如露如電応作如是観
Both those who kill and who are killed are only momentary like dewdrops or lightning. All are an appropriate manifestation, that is the way you should see everything in life

His retainers made death poems too. Among them, Reizei Hangan Takatoyo cut a finger and wrote the following poem with his blood on the wall of the temple:

みよりたつ雲も煙も中空にさそひし風のすゑも残らず

Neither the trailing clouds nor smoke will remain in the end,[23] nor will
the wind which has carried them away into the air

Soon after that, Sue ended up being attacked and killed by Lord Mouri
Motonari.

Article 28

According to an ancient samurai story, there was once a brave general
whose name was Tago-no-Tokitaka, who was from the domain of Iwami.
He was so highly prepared as a general that he never had a heavy or long
night's sleep all through his life. He always used to say to his men, 'Though
man can only live for fifty years, if you do not sleep at night, it would be
worth as much as for 100 years'. Thus he always told his men not to sleep
sluggishly. Therefore, they could not sleep in a relaxing or normal way.

   In my view, as a truly ambitious samurai, you should not like to sleep
deeply, since it can keep you off guard. As in an old saying, 'Rise in early
morning and get to sleep late at night, this is how you should act.'

Also, there are some martial poems on this subject:

とにかくに武士と生て夜を寝るな夜をぬる者は用に立まじ

Anyone who was born as a samurai should not sleep at night. Those
who sleep at night cannot serve very well

らうらうと眠れる武士はなま武士よ真虫ならでは人はささぬぞ

Those samurai who sleep sluggishly are incompetent. If you are not a
mamushi snake[24] you cannot pierce anyone

However, though you should not indulge yourself in sleeping sluggishly
at night you cannot go without sleeping all through your life without
even a short nap from time to time. You should be mindful of this.

---

23   The Japanese word used here is 'Sue' and has the double meaning of 'end' and a
     person's name.
24   A pit viper, here it has double meaning for snakes and 'true samurai', due to its
     similar sound.

However, if you stay awake but become absorbed in drinking, gambling or women, it would be even worse than simply sleeping.

There was a mysterious event one or two years before Tokitaka was ruined. One black kite flew down to the sideboard where Tokitaka's meal used to be prepared and landed there. Tokitaka, seeing this, composed a poem:

とき鷹が朝夕膳をなす棚にとび入るまめは味噌に成るべし

The sideboard is where the meal is prepared for Tokitaka[25] every morning and evening, so if a bean flies onto the meal, it should be brewed into the miso.[26]

Then the kite died at once.

Article 29

According to an ancient samurai story, you should not ride a horse which is beyond your control on the battlefield, as it is embarrassing if, just before commencing an attack, you are struggling to restrain the horse from advancing. You should ride on a horse you can control at your command to go wherever you want to go using the reins with one hand. Take note that a 7- or 8-year-old horse should be fine and that horses that are too young will not do at all. The height of the horse should be 4 shaku, 3 sun [129cm] to 4 shaku, 3 sun and 5 bu [130.5cm]. Do not ride on semi-trained horses. If you ride and stand, you will not match [the horse] in rhythm. When riding a horse in armour, you should ride it in a different way from the one you usually do. Those horses that run well on flat land are preferable, while short-barrelled horses run well in fields and mountains, whereas long-barrelled ones with a high head swim well in rivers.[27]

25   Taka also means 'hawk' in Japanese. Also the word 'tobi' is used here which has the meaning of 'fly' and 'kite'.

26   The play on words here is that the hawk kills the kite; the samurai's name in question refers to the hawk.

27   This story is also found in the 100 military poems of Takenaka Hanbei.

Article 30

According to an old samurai story, the lord of Komatsu Castle in the domain of Kaga was a man named Niwano Gorozaemon-no-Jo Nagashige, who sided with Ishida Jibusho Mitsunari of the West[28] and in Komatsu Castle they prepared for a siege. Supporting them was a man named Yamaguchi Genba-no-kami, who was the lord of Daijoji Castle.

On the other side was a man named Maeda Hizen-no-kami Toshikatsu, the lord of Kanazawa Castle, he was also of Kaga domain, but he was allied with Tokugawa Ieyasu of the East. He left his castle and marched to war on the twenty-sixth day of the seventh month in the year 1600 and in the direction of Echizen. He constructed a fortress on Mt Sanda and had a samurai named Okajima Bicchu-no-Kami stationed there with a troop of 500 men to secure their way through the area of Komatsu and other places. This army had a board of councillors and they decided to assault every enemy castle on their way to Echizen. However, for no apparent reason Maeda Hizen-no-kami Toshikatsu did not attack Komatsu Castle[29] but instead passed through Komatsu on the first day of the eighth month and besieged Daijoji Castle, which was five Ri in distance farther than the castle of Komatsu. [The lord of] Komatsu Castle sent out two troops in different directions, 140 muskets in the direction of Asai and ships with 70 or 80 muskets stationed on an inlet.[30] He assaulted Maeda Hizen-no-kami Toshikatsu's army with these musket troops from the outside and because of this the besieging force fled to the village of Kiba. Meanwhile, the scouts from Komatsu Castle wrongly took their allies as the enemy and reported them as such, which forced the troops from Komatsu to suddenly retreat. In response to this, the other side became spirited and began hammering away with muskets, but at dusk, both sides eventually retreated. On the third day of the month, Maeda's force left that conflict and attacked Daijoji Castle instead. Yamaguchi, who was the lord of Daijoji Castle, with his son, sent ashigaru troops out from the castle to meet them and to fight back. As night fell the Kanazawa side, who were attacking the castle, drove away the castle defenders the next day and broke into the castle town. Here they fought fiercely and countless people died on both sides. Tomita Kurouzu, of the besieging army, was

---

28 This is a reference to the divide between East and West Japan.
29 This castle was considered impregnable.
30 He sends troops out here in two different directions to cover both land and sea.

killed in this battle. Although the besieged in the castle were defending themselves well, they gave way and were confined in the main enclosure towards the end and Maeda Magoshiro Toshikatsu – the attacker – ordered his men to assault from the 'enclosure of the bell' and most soldiers inside the castle were killed. In the end, on the fourth day of the eighth month, Yamaguchi Genba-no-Kami and his son Ukyo-no-Suke – the leaders of the castle defence – killed themselves.

Maeda Magoshiro Toshikatsu – the leader of the attack – and his brother ordered their armies to advance to the West and arrived at a place called Hosorogi, which was on the boundaries of Kaga and Echizen. Meanwhile, Nakagawa Sohan Nyudo, who was kin to Maeda Magoshiro Toshikatsu, intended to advance to Kaga from Osaka and arrived at Tsuruga. However, on hearing that Maeda Magoshiro Toshikatsu had departed for the battle, Otani Gyobu-no-sho tried to block them from advancing by using a fake letter as a ploy. The letter said, 'The army from the West intends to raise a fleet and send it to Kaga.' On discovering this Maeda Magoshiro Toshikatsu was greatly surprised and tried to retreat back to Kanazawa from Hosorogi on the ninth of the eighth month. To make this retreat, Maeda Magoshiro Toshikatsu intended to put his four main retainers, Yamazaki Nagato-no-Kami, Takayama Minamino-bo, Ota Tajima-no-Kami and Cho Kurozaemon-no-Jo, at a place called Gokozuka which would hold the forces of Komatsu Castle at bay while his army retreated past them, allowing them through the castle area. Furthermore, the plan was that, after the main army passed by, the four generals mentioned above, plus their troops, would cross over the tidal beach. Therefore, they put their plan into action and proposed to march along a road called Asai Nawate.[31] Then a young samurai, whose name was Matsudaira Kyubei, came forward from the lower seats[32] and said, 'It is not good to retreat along Asai Nawate, because if we were in that castle, we would not let the enemy simply go if they were passing by our castle along such pathways where footing is not good. Therefore, there is no way that the defenders will simply let us through without attacking. Also, if they do come out and assault, the area around the castle is all muddy and the roads are narrow. If the enemy placed an ambush here and there, while our troops are withdrawing along the narrow path, the enemy can assault with ease and our army will be beaten without doubt.'

31 Nawate means a long straight path between rice fields.
32 Seat order was hierarchical.

Hearing him talk like this, all the veterans said he was too impertinent as a young man and he should rely on their judgment and then they settled on their own plan. They were displeased with the young man and his inappropriate behaviour. However, the old warriors said, if the enemy would come out of the castle to attack them – as the young warrior had warned – then they would be the first ones to defeat them with spears and display actions to show what they, as real warriors, were made of. With this decision in place they left Gokozuka – where they were stationed – at the hour of Snake, which was the morning of the ninth day of the eighth month.

While they were going along the street near the castle, all was quiet and no one came out. Seeing this, every warrior in the troop said to himself that the young samurai Kyubei was wrong as not a single one of the enemy was attacking them.

They came to the narrow path with a width of 2 ken that had muddy rice fields on both sides and when their troops were passing, stretching out along it, the enemy came out of the castle and assaulted them from the rear. The castle troops held down Maeda's side with fierce attacks. The samurai Matsumura Magosaburo, one of the attackers who had come out of Komatsu Castle, made the first sortie; overwhelming the enemy he captured twenty-four enemy heads. The fleeing army were defeated and ran away into the muddy fields as their entire force fell in panic and became dishonourably confused. Then the young warrior, Matsudaira Kyubei, the samurai who expected this situation, went back and became the first one to have a spear fight on the bridge that was upon the road, as did Mizukoshi Nui-no-suke. Other warriors, such as Iwata Denzaemon, Ono Jin'nojo, Inoue Kanzaemon, clashed with spears as well. Then Uesaka Shume also came forward. Also, Haiga Jidayu and Fuwa Mokubei from the Komatsu Castle side were brave and came forward but were killed. Following that, Abiko Sakudayu, Tomita Kohei and Narita Sukekuro fought fiercely in the middle of the bridge. However, the Komatsu castle side were pushed back by 2 or 3 ken from the bridge and seeing this, the army of Kanazawa – the fleeing army – gained momentum and tried to advance to attack. Because of this, Sakuragi Genta, of the Komatsu Castle side, prepared his Horo arrow cape and turned his horse in retreat, thus each side stopped and both began to retreat. While both sides were retreating, Eguchi Saburozaemon – of the fleeing side – went farther on the narrow path, following and observing the enemy for approximately 10 cho and climbed up on a hill and stayed in position for a few hours, observing enemy movements. He returned to the main army in the end. This is what is now called the Battle of Asai Nawate.

Afterwards, there was a reconciliation between both clans, and the two lords met on the twenty-sixth of the ninth month. Prisoners were exchanged on the bridge of Terai Highway and all was completed. Later, whenever he talked about his battles, Toshinaga said the memory of the Battle of Asai Nawate always made him break out in a cold sweat. Toshinaga, the leader of the fleeing force, gave a Kanjo, or letter of appreciation to some who fought with spear in the battle. Most of all, he complimented the young Matsudaira Kyubei and later renamed him Matsudaira Houki-no-Kami.

Among the people of the West, there were some samurai who appealed, as they had heard that the warriors of Kanazawa were being given letters of appreciation, they said that they should receive one too. The lord replied, 'If you ask which side of the bridge the battle ended, the answer would be this, it ended 2 or 3 ken back toward our side. So though the battle actually was initiated in the middle of the bridge, it ended on our side because our allies were outdone in combat, which is why I will not give you a letter of appreciation.'

Article 31

According to an old samurai story, generally speaking, it seems that people compose poems in accordance with their character. With due respect, I will review some poems as follows:

Lord Takeda Shingen's death poem:

大抵還他肌骨好不塗紅粉自風流

Anything in this world will return to its essential quality in the end.
Without putting on makeup (do not put on decorations but be just as you are), it will turn out to be refined

I hear that this lord used to be so gentle in doing everything yet was still devastating when conducting warfare (Yumiya).

Lord Uesugi Kenshin's death poem:

四十九年夢中酔 一期栄花一盃酒
Being drunk in the dream for forty-nine years, a life of prosperity is
nothing more than a cup of sake

I, the author have heard that Kenshin was fearless, fierce and good at
warfare, which I find very likely. The themes of the poems represent so
much of their characters.

Article 32
According to an old samurai story, here are the types of Odoshi, or thongs
and threads that bind the plates of armour together.

Hiodoshi
Red thongs, used for vermilion armour

Itohiodoshi
Red thongs, used for gold armour

Kozakuraodoshi[33]
Purple thread or cord of many colours, used for black armour

Unohanaodoshi
White thread and pale yellow thread to be used on the edges
for silver armour

Kashiraodoshi
Thread of many colours

Araiitoodoshi
A thread of pale pink

(See Figs 15, 16 and 17)

---

33   It is possible that this could have had a cherry blossom pattern.

VOLUME TWO

Article 33
According to an old samurai tale, Lord Takeda Shingen and Lord Tokugawa Ieyasu had a battle in Mikatagahara of Enshu and in the end Lord Ieyasu was defeated and retreated to Hamamatsu Castle.

A retainer of Lord Ieyasu, named Takagi Kyusuke Hiromasa, fought defensively while they all retreated and captured a monk warrior's head and presented it for viewing to the lord.

Having viewed it, Lord Ieyasu said to him, 'Our army consider that we are defeated and everyone in the castle is seriously nervous and unsettled. Show this head to all of them and tell them that you have decapitated Shingen. Tell everyone that our army have won.'

Upon this order, Takagi pierced the head with the tip of his sword and went around saying what he had been told in a loud voice. All the people in the castle, hearing him say this, became enthused and later relaxed with joy.

It is worthy of admiration that Lord Ieyasu had thought of such an excellent idea.

Article 34
According to an old samurai tale, Date Terumune of Sendai intended to put Nihonmatsu Ukyo under his command and attempted to attack him several times while encamped at Shionomatsu. Nihonmatsu was not such a powerful lord but would not surrender. However, as late as the eighteenth of the third month of 1582, Ukyo indicated that he would go to Shionomatsu and surrender. With this offer, Terumune was really pleased and entered into a meeting with him and talked for a while in a relaxed manner, even mentioning that he wanted to rely on him in the future [attempting to secure a peaceful end]. After a while when Ukyo was taking his leave and Terumune came along to see him off, Ukyo took the chance to seize Terumune and held him at sword point by placing the blade on his neck, just like the long dead and famous Benkei warrior monk who took hold of Shozon. In this manner he grabbed Terumune and put him on horseback together with himself. At this point they mounted and rushed back to Nihonmatsu territory.

This event took place while Terumune's son, who was called Masamune,[34] was away. As soon as he heard what had happened, he chased them with a small number and caught up with them at a distance of around 5 or 6 cho of Abukuma River. Masamune killed them all and even killed his own father,[35] he did this so that their attempt to take his father as a prisoner failed. Masamune was only 18 when he did this, but for his young age, he was a very impressive general.

Article 35

According to an old samurai story, a son of Lord Hideyori's nursemaid, Kimura Nagato-no-kami once played a joke on a monk who was serving in Osaka Castle, which was around seven or eight years before the Winter Seige of Osaka Castle. The monk became very angry and said, 'Have at it'. The people who were there were amused but then realised that the situation was going to get increasingly ugly. With this Nagato-no-kami – the prankster – stayed completely calm and returned to his room saying, 'If I did not have something of greater concern, I would not let you go at this point.'

At hearing this, some people said that it was an unexpected development. Others said the monk was in the right. Since then Nagato-no-kami seemed to become introverted each day, while on the other hand the monk was becoming more and more confident and proud.

However, at the time of the Winter Seige of Osaka Castle, Nagato-no-kami performed amazingly well in the battle, attacking Satake's army at Gamo river bank around Shigino. Shibui Naizen – a great samurai general – of the Satake side was killed in this battle. Goto Matabei was astonished to see this spectacular service. The people were impressed with this and said that this action was a reference to the special reason for why he did not fight the monk all those years before. However, Kimura Nagato-no-kami himself stayed modest, even more so and, furthermore, behaved without arrogance. After observing him for a good while, Goto Matabei said, 'He seems to be not satisfied with his own actions in the battle. I think he looks determined to be the first one advancing in the face of death and to do an even greater service next time.'

34 A great tactician known as the 'one eyed dragon'.
35 Presumably he killed his father before he killed the rest of the enemy.

Exactly as Matabei predicted, Kimura Nagato-no-kami fought and died an honourable death at Wakaeguchi. It is said that he honourably faced in the direction of Wakaeguchi, at which point he was decapitated by a 17-year-old samurai, whose name was Ando Chosaburo, a retainer of Ii Kamon-no-Kami Naotaka. Lord Tokugawa Ieyasu viewed the head for inspection; as soon as the head was brought there, a refined fragrance of eaglewood filled the place, as though it was freshly ignited. The lord appreciated this highly, wondering how the young warrior could have been prepared like this.

Article 36

According to an old samurai story, Nagaoka Yusai Fujitaka used to govern Tango domain. One year the people had a crop failure, because of this they asked Fujitaka to make an inspection to observe the severity of it. However, he did not accept their request and in fact did not inspect the crops. In response to this the peasants composed and displayed this poem:

秋の田をからでそのまゝたゞおきのこころながをか何をいふさい
If the rice fields are left as they are without the crop being reaped, what would he say in his mind?[36]

Article 37

According to an old samurai story, there was a samurai whose name was Machino Nagato-no-Kami, who served Gamo Shimotsuke-no-Kami of Aizu. Machino had a renowned warrior named Hattori Den'emon as a retainer, who had decapitated the head of a famous samurai whose name was Oroshi Hikozaemon.

After the death of the lord, a samurai named Kato Sama-no-suke Yoshiaki was given the area of Aizu and came to govern there. As Hattori was then a ronin, he approached the lord to gain employment. However, when hearing that Hattori Den'emon had served Machino Nagato-no-Kami, Sama-no-suke said, 'There seems little

---

36 The words Tadaoki, Nagaoka and Yusai are used here as a play on words, these words are the same as the names of the samurai in question, and the author is using the negatives to reflect Fujitaka's lack of action.

doubt that he got Oroshi's head, but if he was really right-minded in a true sense he would not have been serving Machino Nagato-no-Kami as such a low level retainer. As he had won Orosi's head, he should have been appreciated as incomparably good. However, he was content with such a position probably because he is not such an ambitious samurai.' Therefore, because of this reason, Hattori Den'emon was not employed.

Article 38

According to an old samurai story, a retainer of Lord Gifu Chunagon[37] Hidenobu, also named Kozukuri Taizen, said the following:

No matter how reliable and spirited you think a monk or merchant is, you should not grow too intimate with them, let them know of a grave matter or rely on them in anyway. Essentially, monks and merchants do not do anything that will cause trouble to them and they have little in the way of righteous sense. One or two out of ten may sincere but as a samurai it is not advised to rely on them. When a samurai seems to be feeble-minded, you should still ask them for help, as by this you will be able to feel more secure than if you asked a non-samurai. If your judgment about him turns out to be misguided, it is not a thing to be ashamed of, as you trusted a samurai, even if it was in vain. Also, if you rely on someone who is not so familiar with the way of samurai,[38] no matter how trustworthy and single-minded the monk or merchant, you will not be able to rely on him if the situation turns bad.

Though Lord Takeda Shingen had a fair respect for monks and founded numerous temples in his two domains of Koshu and Shinshu, it turned out that, when his son Lord Katsuyori committed suicide, his head was sent to Kyoto and his body was abandoned along the road where a lot of horses were treading. Not even a single monk from any of those temples would run the risk of going and getting the body for burial, this was because they did not want to arouse the displeasure of Lord Nobunaga.

---

37 Or Oda.
38 武家に不案内の人 – a stranger to samurai.

Furthermore:

The monks of Mt Koya[39] of Kishu domain have changed completely from the way they were in the old days, and they do not shelter any rebel or excommunicate any patron families any more.

The above is even more so with merchants, as they are so undependable, just as grass sways in the wind, therefore there is nothing much to say about them.

Take heed! As a samurai, if you fall into a serious situation and have no one to ask for help, it would be a praiseworthy deed for you to leap to your death into deep water with stones in your sleeves, rather than rely on a monk or merchant, which would be extremely disgraceful.

Article 39

According to an old samurai story, Lord Tokugawa Ieyasu, after he won the Battle of Sekigahara and returned to his castle, had an interview with every allied daimyo and his prominent warriors. Among them, there were three principal retainers attached to Fukushima Saemon-dayu Masanori and they were Fukushima Tanba-no-Kami, Ozeki Iwami-no-Kami and Nagao Hayato-no-Suke. All the three warriors had disabilities. Tango-no-Kami was crippled, Iwami-no-Kami was one-eyed, and Hayato-no-Suke had a hare lip. The interviews were held in the order of Tango, Iwami and Hayato. When Hayato expressed his gratitude in front of the lord, the pages there could not help but burst into uncontrollable laughter. With this, Lord Ieyasu became very angry. He said, 'To every man any disability is no disgrace, while bravery in heart should be held in high esteem. These three warriors are the crème de la crème. You should follow their teaching and set them in your very bones.'

Article 40[40]

According to an old samurai story, this is a list of battles from the past and how many years have been passed from then until now (1654), which I have recorded and kept.

---

39   An alternative name for Kongobuji temple.
40   The original script simply included the date and names as a list, including the number of years between them.

The Battle of Un'noguchi in the province of Shinshu
Eleventh month, 1536 – 119 years ago.

The Battle of Nirasaki in the province of Koshu
Seventh month, nineteenth day, 1538 – 117 years ago.

The Battle of Kawanakajima in the province of Shinshu
Ninth month, tenth day, 1561 – 94 years ago.

The Battle of Konodai in the province of Shimousa
First month, eighth day, 1564 – 91 years ago.

The Battle of Anegawa in the province of Goshu
Sixth month, twenty-eighth day, 1569 – 86 years ago.

The Battle of Mikatagahara in the province of Enshu
Twelfth month, twenty-second day, 1572 – 83 years ago.

The Battle of Nagashino in the province of Sanshu
Fifth month, twenty-first day, 1575 – 80 years ago.

The Battle of Takatenjin in the province of Enshu
1581 – 74 years ago.

The fall of Koshu
Third month, eleventh day, 1582 – 73 years ago.

The Battle of Hon'noji in the province of Joshu (Kyoto)
Sixth month, second day, 1582 – 73 years ago.

The Battle of Takamatsu in the province of Bicchu
1583 – 72 years ago.

The Battle of Shizugatake in the province of Koshu
1583 – 72 years ago.

The Battle of Kaneko in the province of Iyo
1584 – 71 years ago.

The Battle of Komaki in the domain of Bishu
1585 – 70 years ago.

The Battle of Nagakute in the province of Bishu[41]
1585 – 70 years ago.

The Battle of Ueda in the province of Shinshu
1584 – 71 years ago.

The Battle of Sasshuujin
1587 – 68 years ago.

The Battle of Odawara in the province of Soshu
1590 – 65 years ago.

The Battle of Kunohe in the province of Oshu
Tenth month, twenty-fourth day, 1591 – 64 years ago.

The invasion of Korai (Korea)
March, 1592 – 63 years ago.

The Battle of Ueda in the province of Shinshu
Seventh month, 1600 – 55 years ago.

The Battle of Sekigahara in the province of Noshu
September, 1600 – 55 years ago.

The Siege of Osaka Castle in the province of Sesshu
Tenth month, 1614 – 41 years ago.

The fall of Osaka Castle
Fifth month, seventh day, 1615 – 40 years ago.

The Battle of Shimabara in the province of Hizen
Second month, twenty-eighth day, 1638 – 17 years ago.

---

41   This was added in a later edition and did not appear in the original.

Article 41

According to an old samurai story, Amago Haruhisa of Izumo domain fought a battle with Lord Mouri Motonari and was defeated. Afterwards, a defeated chief retainer of the Amago clan, Yamanaka Shika-no-suke, gave backing to a monk – a former Amago samurai – to restart the Amago clan. This monk took the name Amago Katsuhisa, and they held Kozuki Castle. However, it turned out the castle was besieged by Mouri's massive army and was nearly taken. Katsuhisa, just before killing himself, beckoned Shika-no-suke and said, 'My luck has run out. You should survive and surrender to follow Motonari to save the lives of our allies.' Shika-no-suke was surprised with this and strongly insisted on dying with him. To this Katsuhisa said again, 'All depends on you, the fate of many lives of our allies that is. I truly hope you will surrender to Motonari. If you survive, you can wash away the shame of this unendurable disgrace some other day.' Because he strongly requested this action, Shika-no-suke agreed to surrender to Motonari in the end.

Then a messenger was sent from the Mouri side, whose name was Oka Chikuzen. He was a formidable warrior who everybody knew of, even though he was short and ugly looking.

On seeing him, Shika-no-suke said to him, 'Hearing and seeing are very different actually. Now I see you, you do not look as I thought that you, Sir Oka Chikuzen, would look in real life, the man whom I have heard so much about.' And then he laughed. In response to this, the messenger Oka Chikuzen said, 'Sir Shika, you are absolutely right. People are so different when you see them closely, from those facts or judgements you gain only by rumour. I heard that you are one of the greatest warriors that ever existed. I have never imagined that you could suggest to your lord that he should kill himself and then be willing to serve our lord instead. Hearing and seeing are really different things.'

Upon this, Shika-no-suke, though he was a courageous warrior unequalled, cried a tear without saying anything. However, it turned out that soon after Shika-no-suke was killed by some men from the Mouri clan on a ferry boat in Ainowatari of Bicchu.

Article 42

According to an old samurai story, when Lord Tokugawa Ieyasu was at the inspection of the heads of the dead during the Winter Campaign of

Osaka, Honda Sanya came forward and said, 'It is a surprise, but in all these heads you, my lord, have just inspected, I see an omen for reconciliation.' Hearing this, Lord Ieyasu spoke in a temper, 'That is an absurd thing for a mere youngster like you to say. I have come a long way for this battle, how is it possible that I would agree with reconciliation?' However, as Sanya predicted, the winter campaign ended with reconciliation and people rumoured that it was a strange thing. Some people say there are five kinds of heads and it might be the foundation of his prediction.

This above story reminds me of something I should tell:

Recently I had a chance to peruse a manual about head inspection. It lists the types of heads as (See Fig 18):

Right-eyed
Left-eyed
Heaven-eyed
Earth-eyed
Buddha-eyed (half closed)

Could it be that these are the aforementioned five types of heads? Also, there is another type of head, and it is said that it should not be showed to the lord. It also says that there is a way to display a head to public view. On top of that, when you are going to present a Hitotsukubi,[42] or the only head taken during a battle to the lord, there are things you should be aware of.

Here is a copy of a manual for the inspection of heads:
To be prepared for a head inspection, the lord should dress in armour or Kogusoku – which is a type of informal armour. A Tachi long-sword as well as a Katana sword should be worn on the waist. He should hold a folding fan or a round fan in his hand and sit on a chair which is covered with a bear or tiger fur.

The person who is going to show the head should be dressed in full armour with a Yugote,[43] an archer's arm bracer, however they should not don their helmet. The head should be put on a board and it should be

---

42 In a skirmish where only one person dies and only one head is taken.
43 This is a garment to keep the left sleeve of an archer out of the string's way.

held with your thumbs in both ears, holding both the head and the board together, this is to be done crouching but not with your knees on the ground, then show the right side of the head to the lord.

The lord should see it, sitting on his chair, with his right hand on the hilt of the Tachi sword and drawing it just a little, this is done with the spirit of confrontation. Also, this should all be done while looking sideways with the left eye. On top of that, he should have a stance with the left leg forward, as if you were shooting an arrow. Then he should take the fan with the right hand and use it.

The presenter should then withdraw in an anticlockwise direction, holding the board with the head upon it. During the course of the inspection of heads, the lord should wave the fan two or three times.

It goes without saying that if the lord was born in a year of Horse [all will be well, however, if not] put someone who is born in the year of Horse between the lord and the head with a bow of Murashigedo.[44]

On both sides of the head, two Kaburaya[45] arrows, which have the feathers of small birds as fletchings, should be put vertically in the ground. Also, put a strung bow at a distance of 4 shaku from the head, then the lord, in turn, should be 10 shaku away from the bow – making the distance between them 14 shaku.

The warriors attending at both sides and at the rear of the lord should be dressed in armour, with a Tachi drawn and at hand, or they may hold a spear. Their hair should be in the style of Owarawa,[46] just as if you were ready for a battle.

No matter how many heads there are, the lord should inspect no more than seven or eight heads.

About raising a shout of victory:
The one who serves sake should tie up his hair with a twisted paper string. The cup of sake should be filled by pouring the sake into it in four[47] separate gushes, the lord should drink it four times, which makes up sixteen pours

---

44 A Shige is a type of bow which was normally owned by a lord. It is lacquered with rattan rolled around at several points. The Murashigedo, the bow in question here, is similar but with rattan at a fewer number of points.
45 A whistling arrow.
46 A hairstyle with the topknot undone so that a helmet is not obstructed.
47 The number four is the number of death in Japan.

in total. The side dishes that go with the sake should be Awabi abalone, chestnuts and Konbu seaweed.[48] The lord should take up each [of the four] cups for the ceremony and he pours [sake] into them four times in each cup, which adds up to sixteen pours in all and he does not drink from them. Then a shout of victory should be raised three times by the aide. After that, the third in command[49] should recite the last words to the soul of the head.

It is said that Hitotsukubi,[50] or single heads, are not to be shown to the lord. However, if the lord would like to see it, he can see it by following the proper procedures.

The five types of the heads are: right-eyed, left-eyed, heaven-eyed, earth-eyed and Bhudda-eyed heads. Another type is the head of hatred, that is, those heads which are distorted and set grimacing, left-eyed and with a clenching of the teeth. In this case the 'Kubimatsuri', or mass, for the repose of the soul of the dead, should be held.

The ritual spell to be chanted at the inspection of heads:

諸悪本末無明来実検直儀何処有南北
'Shoaku honmatsu mumyourai jikken chokugi kashoyu nanboku'

If it is chanted, the dead will immediately attain Buddha-hood and enlightenment, this is done so that you will not be cursed or given over to divine punishment.

Only one person in the clan should read the descriptions of heads. He should read at the right side of the lord. Generally, the enemy heads should not be brought within the castle.

The board for a head should be 8 sun square. It should have a nail to fix the head in place and the corners should be rounded off, one tradition says it should be made of Chinaberry wood.

When the inspection is finished, the side dishes and sake should be offered to the lord. One of the 'head presenters' should be chosen and given a cup of sake. (See Fig 19.) The way to arrange the side dishes is the same as that for the return of the lord. A shout should be given only once.

---

48 The three things represent defeat, victory and joy respectively, this is once more a play on words.
49 Gunkan.
50 Hitotsukubi literally means 'one head', which is the only head taken in battle.

For immediate and informal occasions, you (or the lord) can see the heads while standing, but with the right hand on the hilt of your sword and with the left foot remaining down, then you should put your right foot ahead of the left, and you are to have only a glimpse at the head sideways and only using the left eye. The spell to be chanted is the same as above.

The inscription for the enemy head:
The head container should have a lid. Write an inscription on the lid. The inscription should have his name, title and other things. The ideograms should be in Kaishyo, that is, block style writing.

The heads of those of a high position should be put in containers, with the names written on the lid, not with a tag on the head itself. Also around the container a sutra, or invocation, should be written.

The container should be 1 shaku, 5 sun high, 8 sun in diameter and have a swastika drawn on the cover. Sew two pieces of fabric together and wrap the container and secure it at the top. When the container is sent, put a Kibo arrow across under the knot of the box.

The tag to be put on the head:
It should be made of cedar wood and be 4 sun long, 7 bu wide, with the tip angled like a playing piece in Shogi Japanese chess. Put a string to it and put it through the left earlobe. Write the name they are commonly known by and also their personal name on it.

Washing the heads:
Wash from the lower people's heads first. Then attend to the hair. If it is a head of position, comb the hair and tie it with a paper twisted string. If a head of lower ranking, just tie it with a left-handed rope[51] of 1 shaku, 4 sun. Tie it in a tight knot without making any loops.

To send the head to the enemy, join two pieces of silk, 2 shaku long, and place the head at the centre and then tie the four corners of the cloth. Then put it into a container.

Before sending it back, you should have your men fall into rank behind the head at a distance of 5 jo [15m]. Then, the men raise only one shout of victory. With this cry the head can be sent out. This is also done at the end of any head inspection.

---

51   Normally ropes were right-handed.

The enemy heads should be thrown away in the direction of Shikan 死喚.[52]

On the days of Rat, Horse, Hare, and Cockerel the ninth direction from Hare is to be used.

On the days of the Ox, Ram, Dragon and Dog the ninth direction from Dragon is to be used.

On the days of Tiger, Monkey, Snake and Boar the ninth direction from Snake is to be used.

Take the heads in these directions above and gibbet them, this will make the heads call their fellows[53] and kill them, for they want company [in death]. These gibbeted heads should be avoided at all costs.

If there are evil people in the direction of Shikan, you should kill them and their heads should be thrown away in the ninth direction from Hare, Dragon or Snake.

Concerning the wood to be used for a gibbet:

The heads of aristocrats and generals should be gibbeted on chestnut wood while the lower rank heads should be on pear tree wood. When a number of heads are gibbeted, put up a chestnut wood post on the right and a pear wood on the left, then put silk tree wood across them. The head of the general [or Lord] should be wrapped in a Horo arrow cape when gibbeted. This is called Buddha-gake.

The stands where the heads should be put:

If it is a noble man's head, the stand should be a Kugyo, that is a board with a brim and footed. The lower rank should have an Ashi-no-Uchi, or footed stand, and even lower ranks should have a Kan'nakake board without feet.

Kubikakenawa rope is used to hold the head, this can be made from the cord of a quiver. If not a quiver, a Hachimaki head band or a sash from armour will be fine. How to hold it is to be orally transmitted.

The heads of lower ranking people should be made in the Tabusa[54] hairstyle with a left-handed rope and also they should be tied up [to the gibbet] with this rope. This way is called Hiroikake.

---

52 This is a direction that changes dependent on the day and moves in accordance with Chinese astrology.

53 i.e., the enemy army.

54 A handful of hair on top of the head bunched up and tied.

According to the degree of their crime, some heads should be paraded around the streets, and/or gibbeted. There are traditions to be kept for each case. In the case where you are in a battlefield and present a head to the lord while carrying a bow: first hide the head and put your bow on the ground with the string toward the lord to make it a threshold. Then show the head to the lord. After that, hide it on the other side and withdraw with your bow.

How to carry heads on horseback:
Put them on the left horn of the Shiode[55] by dividing the topknot and tying it there. If you get two heads, put the second onto the right saddle-horn.

How to record the heads; an example:
From the Battle of 'Tensho seven' (1579) Tsuchinoto U (year of the Hare), on the fifth day of the seventh month in the hour of Snake (9-11 a.m.)

Descriptions of the decapitated heads:
'Oumamawari[56] – the lord's mounted guard'

Put a space between the two parts below. The lower[57] part[58] should be written in fine line and thin colour, while the upper part in fine line but thick colour.[59]

One head, Watabe Hyozaemon [insert a space here] killed with a Tachi by Yamada Jibuzaemon.

One head, [insert name & position] [insert a space here] killed with a spear by [insert name & position]

Yamashita Sukezaemon [insert a space here] captured alive by Morita Sasuke.

---

55 A string attached to the saddlebows on both sides.
56 This is a heading, no pun intended, to show which unit took the heads in battle.
57 The name goes at the top and the killer at the bottom. These were records written in the Japanese style of right to left, top to bottom.
58 i.e., the name of the killer.
59 i.e., a thick ink.

One head [insert name & position] [insert a space here] killed with Tachi together by [name & position] & [name & position].

One head [name & position] [insert a space here] killed with a Tachi by [name & position] with the help of [name & position].

[An example recording a group of heads]:
Heads taken by the troop led by Akimoto Yemon
The heads should be written in the same style as above.
More than 2,100 heads were taken, including more than 100 people caught alive. On top of that, a countless number were killed in pursuit.

Write as above on Sugihara paper or some other form of proper paper. Folded styles of paper will also be fine. Only the first, second and third heads should be recorded as well as the generals' heads. The fourth and fifth heads should be [socially] less important. However, it all depends on the situation.

How to write the names of the dead when you send their heads back to the enemy:

Insert date [at the top right]
From Ikeda Juzaemon [under the date]
[Sent to] Sir Kondo Hanzaemon [top left but below the date]

Put a space between your name and the enemy name just like the space between the head that has been cut off.[60]
If you get a letter like this from the enemy, you have to write something in the space just after the date. This is a very important secret to be passed down.

This is the end of the writing on the inspection of heads.

Article 43
According to an old samurai story, the twenty-fifth generation from Prince Taira-no-Masakado, who was named Soma Daizen-no-kami

---

60   A reference to decapitation.

Toshitane, had a retainer named Kanazawa Bicchu. His family had served the Soma clan generation after generation. By the time of Kanazawa Bicchu, as many as eleven generations of his family had been killed in battle in front of their lord's horse. Bicchu had a son, Kanazawa Chubyoe. When the twenty-sixth inheritor of the Soma clan, Lord Daizen-no-kami Yoshitane, was dying because of illness, he said, 'Eleven generations including my father have died for faith in front of the lord's horse. However, I have done nothing to serve this lord in such a manner; no need has arisen during my generation in the service of our lord Daizen. If there is one thing I can do, it would be to follow the lord on the journey to the other world.'

Then he killed himself. Indeed, it is said that there are few samurai families who have died in the service of a lord for twelve generations.

Article 44

According to an old samurai story, there was a place named Yamazato in the area within Ota Dokan's castle. Once, a huge umbrella-shaped mushroom sprouted out. Everyone said it was a kind of evil spirit and told Dokan. On hearing this, Dokan said, 'It is not an evil spirit or such, if it sprouted out upside down, then it might be so. However, it is just bigger than the usual ones.' He then paid it no more attention.

About twenty days after he said this, a similar mushroom sprouted out again but upside down this time. Everyone was surprised to see this and told Dokan. He said, 'As I said before it would be strange if it grows upside down, it must have picked up what I said, so there is no wonder that it has come out upside down,' and then he laughed.

Later on, it so happened that a hearth stand danced around a room laid with Tatami mats. To see this, Dokan said, 'Human beings can walk with only two feet. No wonder it can walk as it has three feet! This kind of thing always happens by chance and people easily get anxious and disturbed.' He did not care for it at all and nothing else took place thereafter.

Article 45

According to an old samurai story, there was a samurai whose name was Matsuda Kinshichiro Hidenobu, who was a retainer of Tentokuji Munetsuna Nyudo in Sano of the domain of Shimotsuke. He was born in Yamato. His master, Tentokuji Munetsuna Nyudo found and employed him when he went up to Kyoto, because it was known that he was an samurai who had achieved much.

Kinshichiro possessed such a phenomenal strength that he used to march with a huge twelve-layered Horo[61] arrow cape with large bird feathers and carrying a gold covered deer horn as a standard.

After his lord died, Kinshichiro Hidenobu was employed by Gamo Ujisato and then after Ujisato died, Kinshichiro was attached to the troop of Natsuka Okura-no-tayu at the Battle of Sekigahara. At the battle he captured and dragged in ten of the enemy with a rake and had his allies cut off their heads, then he himself was killed in the battle.

Article 46

According to an old samurai story, at the Winter Siege of Osaka Castle, Suzukida Hayato-no-suke, who was on the side of Lord Hideyori, was given command of a ship to defend against the central west provinces and he was stationed at Etsuda Castle. However, Hachisuka Awa-no-kami, from Ieyasu's side, attacked and captured the castle so Hayato-no-suke fled to Osaka to save his life.

The next spring, when Lord Hideyori's senior counsellors met together to talk about strategies, this Suzukida was also present. Then a 12- or 13-year-old page boy went to him with a large fruit called an Okoji and said, 'Look at this sir Hayato-no-suke. Do you not think it is a beautiful fruit?' To this, he agreed that it was quite beautiful. Then the boy said, 'This big Okoji fruit is just like you Sir Hayato-no-suke, if it were a human that is. It looks so graceful but it is not quite so on the inside, therefore, it cannot be served as food. Remember, you cannot judge things by their looks alone.'

At which the defeated samurai Hayato-no-suke was terribly embarrassed. However, at the Summer Siege, on the sixth of the fifth month, he was killed magnificently at the Domyoji entrance to the castle and his head was cut off by Kawakami Shinpachiro, a retainer of Mizuno Hyuga-no-kami Katsunari.

It is said the page boy was told to speak as such by Ono Shuri-no-suke.

---

61   A defensive cape to deflect arrows.

Article 47

According to an old samurai story, there is a song sung by local people in Mikawa which they sing while grinding with a hand mill. It goes thus:

徳川様はよい人もちよ 服部半蔵は鬼半蔵　渡辺半蔵は鑓半蔵
渥美源五は首取源五

Lord Tokugawa has good men. Hattori Hanzo[62] is the Devil Hanzo, Watanabe Hanzo is Spear Hanzo and Atsumi Gengo is the Head-Taker Gengo.

Article 48

According to an old samurai story, Date Masamune of Sendai fell into discord with his former ally Ashina Morishige of Aizu, and allied with himself Inawashiro Moritane, the lord of Inawashiro Castle who was also from Aizu, and they went to battle with Ashina Morishige in the middle of the Tensho period (1589). The vanguard, including Haneda Inaba-no-kami, Katakura Kojuro, Date Awa-no-kami and so on, and numbered at around 3,000 people, were encamped in Suriagehara. The Hatamoto command group stayed on Mt Bandai. Seeing this, Ashina Morishige – the defender – said to all his men, 'We will not come back to our castle unless we win a victory in this battle with Masamune. Observe our determination!' And from here they entered into combat with the attackers. When all of his army had crossed over the Niihashi River, they set fire to the bridge and encamped with the river to the rear. The purpose of this action was to show his determination to everyone that there would be no chance of retreat and the safety of the castle unless they had victory. However, Morishige intended to position an army of 10,000 people in Suriagehara but his four principle retainers, Sayo, Tomita, Hirata and Matsumoto betrayed him and secretly took the side of Sendai the attacker. Morishige was anxious to begin a battle but the four treacherous retainers would not mobilise their troops and he could not help but spend quite a few days dealing only with foot soldier skirmishes.

---

62   This is the famed Hattori Hanzo, shinobi leader and aid to Tokugawa Ieyasu, he is often confused with Spear Hanzo owing to him receiving a spear as a gift from the Shogun.

Eventually Morishige went to attack the front of the invader Masamune with his main retainers. Meanwhile, Masamune secretly moved with his army centre from Mt Bandai across the river at Dojima and succeeded in capturing the castle. On getting the signal to confirm this capture, Masamune's vanguard started to fight fiercely against Morishige's defending army. Although Morishige was resolute in battle, because of the betrayal of these four retainers, his army was defeated.

A son of Tomita – a senior retainer of the defending side – who was a Shogun imperial guard, said, 'Even though my father betrayed him, I have no dishonesty,' and after saying this he went deep across the enemy line, killed a samurai named Taromaru Kamon and brought his head to show his lord.

Afterwards, Morishige's Castle was taken by Masamune. As Morishige was the youngest son of Satake Yoshiakira – a powerful warlord – he withdrew to his home domain of Hitachi, he changed his name to Yorihiro and lived in Ryugasaki of Hitachi. Though he was a son of Satake, he took the name Morishige as it was a noble family name of Aizu.

VOLUME THREE

Article 49

According to an old samurai story, Lord Ouchi Yoshitaka had a woman whom he loved and paid visits to in secret. Once, he sent a letter by messenger but the messenger heard him wrong and delivered it to his wife. Reading this letter, the wife made a poem and sent it to the woman.

頼むなよ行末かけて替わらじと我にもいひしことのはのすゑ

Do not rely on him or his feelings towards you, he says he will not change but that's what he used to say to me

After that, she also sent a poem to her lord as well:

思ふこと二つありその浜千鳥踏みちがへたる跡こそみれ

It seems the plover bird must have had two different things in mind. You can see its footsteps stray from the path

Article 50

According to an old samurai story, the lord of Daijoji Castle in Kaga domain, Yamaguchi Genba-no-Kami allied himself with Ishida Mitsunari and defended the castle against a siege but in the end yielded at last to Maeda Toshiie, who was on the side of Lord Ieyasu.[63] Toshiie reported the incident to the Lord Ieyasu. In reply, Lord Ieyasu appointed Horio Tatewaki, who was also the lord of Hamamatsu Castle in Enshu, with the defence of the newly aquired Daijoji Castle. There was another castle near to Hamamatsu, called Kariya Castle and Mizuno So-byoe-no-jo was its lord. As their castles were closely located, the two lords often met for friendly talks at Chiryu within Mizuno's domain.

One time they met up in Chiryu to talk about the task of defending the acquired Daijoji Castle. Then during this talk a samurai, whose name was Kaganoe Yahachiro, who sympathised with the defeated Ishida Mitsunari, came to Chiryu and was outfitted for a long journey. The two lords saw

---

63   See Volume One, Article 30.

this and asked him where he was going. Yahachiro replied that he intended to join them and to side with Ieyasu and that he was going down to Kanto region. They questioned the travelling samurai Yahachiro, saying they thought he was allied with Ishida and that it must be a lie or that he had an ill intention. He replied that was what other people had said but it was his true intention to side with them and their lord and that he had given a solemn oath. To this they said, 'Then your word must be true. However, as you are not so highly ranked, you will be of little use to Lord Ieyasu. Therefore we will communicate to Kanto about your intentions; and you should not proceed but in fact wait for an answer in reply.' They also said, 'As Sir Tatewaki is going to take charge of Daijoji Castle, it is probably best that you should go there with him.' The travelling samurai Yahachiro replied that he would leave everything to them and agreed to go to the castle.

On hearing this, the two samurai were pleased and had a boisterous party filled with booze and revelry. In the middle of the party the new, travelling samurai, Yahachiro, drew his sword and killed the lord So-byoe-no-jo, and tried to kill Tatewaki as well. However, Tatewaki drew his sword and after a hard fight killed the traitor samurai in the end. Once So-byoe-no-jo's men came and saw this, they mistakenly thought that Tatewaki had betrayed So-byoe-no-jo and had killed both him and the new, and lower samurai, Yahachiro (who was the real traitor). Twenty to thirty people now attacked him with swords and Tatewaki defended himself by fighting with them until he could get back to his men and explain what happened. At which point, a page who was attending the party, who knew what had happened, told his side of the story, and thus it was revealed that Lord Tatewaki was indeed telling the truth.

Afterwards, when looking into the traitor Yahachi's pouch, there was a signed deed from Ishida's side. It says that if he killed both Mizuno So-byoe-no-jo and Horio Tatewaki, he was promised to be given both their domains of Mikawa and Enshu.

Article 51
According to an old samurai story, there are six tools for a Musha warrior.

A Horo: an 'arrow-catching cape' which is shaped like a placenta, a shape that makes it worthy, as it is the result of the combination of In and Yo (Yin and Yang). This tool will protect you from any disaster.

A quiver: this quiver is modelled after the head of a demon called Isora.[64] The deity Taishakuten killed this demon with twenty-five arrows, Therefore, a samurai's quiver should have twenty-five arrows in it. There is one arrow which is most important. This single arrow is used to change a direction from an unlucky one to a positive one.

Archers' sleeve:[65] this represents Kongokai[66] and Taizokai. Details are omitted.

A small flag: used to display a family crest. This is to display your surname without having to announce it. There are details to be known about this flag.

A folding fan: it should have ten ribs which represent the ten great virtues in Buddhism. In our country these ten great virtues symbolise the great Bodhisattva, Hachiman Daibosatsu, remember, there is nothing more suitable for a Bushi warrior to worship than this.

A rod or whip: this represents the twenty-eight lunar mansions in Chinese astronomy. The whip should be 2 shaku, 7 sun long, this represents twenty-seven of the mansions. You yourself represent one mansion, which adds up to a total of twenty-eight. Its construction should be orally transmitted.

The above are called the Rokugu or six tools.

Article 52

According to an old samurai story, Sendai Chunagon[67] Masamune was one-eyed and composed his death poems as follows:

照一眼向琰王云　我者是奥州守

64　The meaning of this word is unknown.

65　Heiju 兵拾 – not found in modern Japanese, most likely the sleeve that holds back the archer's top to stop the string from catching on it.

66　The Dainichikyō 大日経 is a form of Sutra which contains these two references. Kongokai 金剛界曼荼羅 or Diamond World and Taizokai 胎蔵界曼荼羅 or Womb/World are forms of Mandala. It appears that the author meant that the item in question represented these two concepts.

67　Or Date.

With one shining eye I declare to the king of Hell that I am the Lord
of Oshu

曇なき心の月をさき立て浮世の闇を照してぞ行く
By lighting ahead with the clear moon in my mind I have made my way
in the darkness of this world

Article 53

According to an old samurai story, there were two bright samurai serving
Kato Sama-no-suke Yoshiaki, whose names were Kawagi Gorozaemon
and Kurokawa Kahyoe. Among all the retainers, these two were the most
deeply determined on the path of samurai – that is Bushido. So much so
that everyone complimented them, saying they would distinguish themselves as warriors in due course.

Of these two, Kawagi was always trying to outdo Kurokawa while
Kurokawa was also trying to do better than Kawagi. At the coming of the
Winter Siege of Osaka, these two warriors left, accompanying the lord's
son Shikibu Shosho[68] to battle. During the journey they had to cross
over the Yodo River. Realising this, the two came to step into the river
on horseback and had their horses swim side by side. Unfortunately, the
other side afforded no footing and the horses could not get out of the
river and both the men and horses drowned. Everyone grieved for them
with clenched fists, thinking that it was a tragic death.

There was another brave samurai, who was a retainer of the above and
now dead Kawagi. He told his wife and children, 'Now our master leaves
our domain, I think he will not come back again. If it is the case, then
neither will I.' As he predicted, he followed his master and he stepped
into the river and tried to swim across holding his horse's tail, but he was
also drowned.

Also, Kurokawa used to tell his horse in advance of combat, 'As I treas-
ure you so much I totally trust you to be of true value if the occasion so
arises. If things turn out against my wishes we will die together. Please do
not think ill of me for this.' True to his word, he stabbed his horse twice
at the side of the neck while they were both in the water. That is what
was found after the bodies were raised from the deep.

---

68   Also known as Kato Akinari.

Article 54

According to an old samurai story, in the domain of Echigo, Lord Nagao Tamekage had two sons, named Sir Rokuro and Sir Sarumatsu.[69] Rokuro was very gentle while Sarumatsu was extraordinarily mischievous. Lord Tamekage disliked Sarumatsu and expelled him from Echigo at the age of 12 or 13 years. Later on, the lord was killed in a battle with the enemies of Kaga and Ecchu, and his son Rokuro succeeded his father.

However, since he was so gentle he spent time without the intention to fighting a battle to avenge his father's death and it made the enemies in neighbouring provinces overconfident and they tried to invade Echigo. Then, Sir Sarumatsu, the mischievous child, who had been roaming the land, heard of that and came back home without delay. He raised the allied army and won a victory over the enemies in both Kaga and Ecchu. Even though he achieved his aim, the retainers of the clan did not have much attachment to him due to his wandering and no one raised the issue of whether Sir Sarumatsu should be the head of the clan.

Therefore, Sir Sarumatsu said, 'Now that I have fought an avenging battle for my father, there is nothing to regret and now as I have something to think about, I will go up to Mt Koya of Kishu and become a priest.' The retainers greatly surprised to hear this and tried to stop him, but he went as far as two or three Ri from the castle. There the retainers followed him and said, 'Please stay with us. If you do not then our domain of Echigo will be taken by the enemy.' He replied to this, 'Then will you follow my orders from now on?' They agreed to it, so he told them to take an oath and thus he came back with them. After that he defeated or killed[70] those who would not take his side, forcing his brother Sir Rokuro to retire and making himself the lord of Echigo. It was this Sir Sarumatsu who later became Lord Nagao Kenshin Terutota.[71]

---

69 Kenshin's childhood name was Torachiyo. There was an elder brother of Kenshin named Saruchiyo, however he died young. It is considered to be the author's mistake here.

70 Here the word Seibai 成敗 is used, this can mean defeat but has connotations of execution.

71 He was a famed samurai of the Sengoku period who opposed Takeda Shingen, and was considered a great tactician.

Article 55

According to an old samurai story, there was a very brave samurai named Shino-no-Saizo, who was a retainer of Fukushima Saemon-dayu Masanori. During the Battle of Sekigahara in 1600, Saemon-dayu sent him, together with another younger samurai, as messengers. The younger one said, 'Let's go along outside of the Taketaba bamboo shields.' To this Saizo replied, 'There is a hail of bullets and arrows on the outside, thus I cannot accompany you.' So he went inside the shield wall. The younger samurai took the outside route saying, 'What does it matter if you go along the outside?' Favoured with good luck he succeeded in arriving at the destination without being shot. As the older samurai Saizo had taken the inside route, he arrived there without event or problem. After they regrouped and delivered the message to the receiver and made preparations to return, the young and 'brave' samurai said in a scared tone, 'You were correct in your judgement, Sir Saizo. The arrows and gunshots from the enemy were so fierce that I scarcely survived.'

To hear that, Saizo said, 'Though I hoped to go with you at the start, we had been told to deliver an important message, if we were killed before successfully passing it to the receiver, it would have gone against the military laws. Now we are finished with the mission, there will be no problem if we are killed by an arrow or gunshot.' Thus, he insisted on taking the outside route while the young warrior went on the inside of the shields. Saizo came back without being shot.

Article 56

According to an old samurai story, those who have decapitated some famous generals or warriors are listed here; as I have remembered them.

Lord Imagawa Yoshimoto was decapitated by Mori Shinsuke.
Torii Shirozaemon was decapitated by Tsuchiya Yemon-nojo.
Baba Mino-no-kami was decapitated by Kawai Sanjuro.
Naito Shuri-no-suke was decapitated by Asahina Sozaemon.
Oda Shichibyoe was decapitated by Ueda Mondo-no-suke.
Ikeda Shonyu was decapitated by Nagai Ukon.
Ikeda Shokuro was decapitated by Ando Tatewaki.
Mori Shozo was decapitated by Honda Hachizo.
Kawajiri Yohyoe was decapitated by Mitsui Yaichiro.

Shinagawa Okami-no-suke was decapitated by Yamanaka Shika-no-suke.
Yamanaka Shika-no-suke was decapitated by Kawaya Shinzaemon.
Hojo Tango-no-kami was decapitated by Ogita Shume.
Sanada Saemon-no-suke was decapitated by Nishio Nizaemon.
Mishuku Echizen-no-kami was decapitated by Nomoto Ukon.
Kimura Nagato-no-kami was decapitated by Ando Chosaburo.
Susukida Hayato-no-suke was decapitated by Kawamura Shinpachiro.
Akashi Kamon-no-suke was decapitated by Migiwa San'emon.
Ban Dan'emon was decapitated by Yagi Shinzaemon.
Orosi Hikozaemon was decapitated by Hattori Den'emon.

Article 57

According to an old samurai story, samurai should always wish to keep to the righteous path or shodo, 正道, and try not to fall into the way of depravity, even if it is difficult to accomplish.

Those samurai who keep on with the right path will achieve high honours with the aid of Buddha and the gods, while those who have fallen into a corrupt way will naturally meet with misfortune and be laughed at by the people of the world.

For instance, Lord Tokugawa Ieyasu was not always so powerful and was once held as hostage by Lord Imagawa Yoshimoto. In time, Lord Yoshimoto was destroyed by Lord Oda Nobunaga, which left Yoshimoto's heir, Ujimasa, in command, but he was defeated by Lord Takeda Shingen and had to relinquish Sunpu.

At that time, Lord Ieyasu's brother, Sir Genzaburo and Ofu, who was the daughter of one of his chief retainers, Sakai Saemon-no-jo, were also held as hostages within the Imagawa clan. A samurai named Miura Yoji took them away, and instead of taking them back to Lord Ieyasu as he should have done, he took them to Koshu and passed them to Lord Shingen, he did this as Lord Shingen was the most powerful presence at the time and was winning every battle and it was reputed that soon he would conquer the whole country.

However, soon after that Lord Shingen died and the Takeda clan collapsed and Lord Ieyasu destroyed Lord Shingen's heir, Lord Katsuyori and this act allowed Ieyasu to prosper.

Miura Yoji, the man who had betrayed the hostages fell into a difficult predicament and ended up becoming a vagabond.

This is exactly what he invited upon himself by moving onto the path of evil. As Genzaburo and Ofu were offered as hostages by Lord Ieyasu, if Miura Yoji was a right-minded warrior, he would have taken them to Mikawa, no matter what the situation. However, he had an evil desire deep within his mind, and because he did this thing, he got his comeuppance.

Article 58

According to an old samurai story, a samurai whose name was Mukai Noto-no-kami said:

To hold and decapitate an enemy, pin him down by sitting astride him, keeping his dominant arm firmly under your right foot,[72] turn up his Shikoro helmet neck plates and then stab and cut the throat first, and then hold your Wakizashi short-sword with a reverse grip, move the head into place[73] by holding the Miagenoita helmet peak and cut off the head.

Article 59

According to an old samurai story, there are various writings about the origin of the Horo arrow catching cape:

During the reign of the Han Dynasty in ancient China, General Su Wu was ordered to conquer the barbarians of Hu and advanced on them. However, the barbarians were so strong that Su Wu was captured and had the tendon of one leg cut and was made to herd sheep in a land of snow for nineteen years. A poem was made by or for him saying, 'When thirsty, I drink drops from a cave and when hungry, I eat snow from heaven.' He was allowed to have a Horo cape as it is said that the Horo cape is to protect you in both this world and in the next. Therefore, Su Wu put a message onto the wing of a goose with the cord of Taishaku[74] of his Horo, by sending his letter in this manner, he finally returned to his homeland. That is why, traditionally,

---

72 Most likely foot and not leg because of the use of the verb *fumaeru*.

73 The sentence here is unclear, it is either to remove the peak of the helmet or to remove the helmet by the peak, or even to move the head into position by holding the peak.

74 It is unknown what this is, it appears to be a part of the Horo arrow-cape.

one cord of the Taishaku is shorter than the other. Su Wu used the ideogram 幌[75] for Horo.

In addition, in ancient China, Fan Kuan was a retainer of Gao-zu of the Han Dynasty. During the Chu versus Han contention, Gao-zu was defeated seventy-four times. When Gao-zu left for the seventy-fifth battle, Fan Kuan made his farewell to his mother and she in a fond farewell said, 'You should imagine you were in my womb' and cover your armour with silk fabric. He did this and the fabric protected him and he achieved great deeds and came back to see his mother again. That is why the ideogram for Horo is 母衣 meaning mother and clothes.

According to Kagakushu,[76] the word Horo has come from the placenta of a mother's womb, which the baby has on its head and it protects the baby from various kinds of harm. Therefore, when a warrior goes to battle, if he fights the enemy with a Horo cape covering him, it protects him from harm, just like the placenta does. A mother's womb and a battlefield are the times of your birth and your death.

Zhang Liang was also a retainer of the Emperor Gao. Before going to war, he visited his father and mother's grave, where he found ivy on his parents' tomb. He kept it on his armour while fighting in battle. He won the battle as he wished. Therefore, the writing for Horo also can have the ideogram for ivy, as in this example 武蘿.

This is an ancient saying:

It is polite conduct for those who pass by Mt Li to pray at the grave of the first emperor. Why would there not be any response if you visit your father and mother's grave?[77]

The container for the Horo cape is the one mentioned in the chapter Kyoikusa in Volume 33 of the great *Taiheiki* war chronicle. (See Fig 20)

Nasu-no-Goro was determined to die in battle and sent a message with a messenger to his old mother that he had left back home. However, she did not show grief but said in her reply, 'Once born into a samurai

---

75 The word Horo has several ideograms and variations.
76 A Japanese dictionary completed in 1444.
77 The point here is that Zhang Liang prayed at his parents' grave and got an answer, thus so should all others.

family, it is usual to value your fame rather than your life. You should be prepared to throw away your life not to disgrace our ancestors. I include in this reply the Horo arrow cape which once belonged to Nasu-no Yoichi[78] – one of our ancestors. He wore this during the Battle of Yashima and achieved fame by hitting his targets with his arrows.' When she finished, she gave him a red Horo cape in a bag of gold brocade. This one was the same as the one mentioned at the start of this article.

Article 60

According to an old samurai story, Lord Hojo Ujiyasu and his heir and son, Lord Ujimasa, shared a meal. Upon seeing his son eat, Lord Ujiyasu began shedding tears and said: 'The Hojo family, our clan will end with my life.' At this the atmosphere was ruined and not only the Lord Ujimasa, but also all his chief councillors had a depressed look about them. Then the lord Ujiyasu said, 'Look at how my son Ujimasa is taking his meal, he has put some soup onto his bowl of rice, then he has added more. Every single person, noble or humble, eats two meals every day, so it cannot be possible that he is not well trained at this. It is such poor judgement that he cannot properly estimate the amount of soup that you should put in your bowl of rice and that he needs to take more, as if it was not enough. He does not have the basic judgement for even a routine task as this, one that is done every morning and evening; therefore, he could never evaluate someone and discover what he is really thinking about, deep inside under the surface. If he does not have this ability, then he cannot recruit good samurai. If he does not have good samurai under his command in this time of war, it is obvious that, if I die tomorrow, the clever lords of the neighbouring domains will invade us and ruin my son Ujimasa. I am afraid this is the truth. Thus our Hojo clan will end with my life.'

Article 61

According to an old samurai story, at the Winter Siege of Osaka, Ban Dan'emon led a night attack on the camp of Hachisuka Awanomori of the East. The troops on the flank were led by Komeda Kenmotsu and the

---

78   The famous archer who hit the fan on top of the mast of a boat at the Battle of Yashima.

rear troop was led by a ronin of Harima named Yamada Gorozaemon. It was known that Ban was the commander of the night attack because he had wooden plates scattered along the way that said 'the commander of this night attack is Ban Dan'emon'.

Afterwards, at the Summer Siege of Osaka, he was killed in Kashinoe village in Izumi. A stone monument for him still exists there. The head of Dan'emon was decapitated by Yagi Shinzaemon, who was from Asai Kii-no-Kami's clan.

Article 62

According to an old samurai story, when you are going on a march with a number of people, if the wind is against you and strong, blowing into your faces, then you should encamp in a place chosen carefully. Also, if the wind is in your face do not rush to do battle, however, if the wind is behind you or blows from your right side, you should stay on the march no matter how strong the wind is.

What to do in case you find the enemy desperate: for example, if they burn down their ships even though they have a river at hand, burn their own rations, or throw away pots and kettles, you should know they are determined to fight until the bitter end.[79] Even if they are a small number, you should not set upon them immediately. You should wait for days to tire them out, or try for arbitration and defeat them by taking advantage of a gap if they show any.

For night attack, you should choose a stormy night, one with a strong wind and strong rain. At such a time you should be thorough about passwords and Aijirushi identifying marks. When you go across the enemy line in the night, tie up the horses' tongs with cloth, cover or roll things that may make sounds, such as the iron fittings of the horse bits, handles, etc. and when withdrawing from this night attack, you should retreat with archers or riflemen at the rear [of your retreat]. The reason is, if the enemy try to hold you in check, you may have to fight them back.

If you see armoured warriors in the bush and birds are not startled and even perch in the area, you should know they are fake. Old tradition says if flying birds are not startled above a fortress, you should know the enemy is trying to deceive you with fake figures.

---

79   Literally, 'one life in ten deaths'.

In the event of a fire in your camp, everyone should stick to his own position in the camp. Do not leave your post to try to fight the fire recklessly. Only the troop at the location of the fire should be in charge of fire fighting. In the case where the fire spreads too much, only then should other troops in that area work together. Even if there is a parent or son involved in the fire, you should never go into where a fire is raging.

Oan Monogatari, The Story Of Oan and of Okiko, Seventeenth Century

1   Oan is not a person's name but is presumed to mean 'an old nun'.

The children came and said, 'Wise nun, please tell us an old story,' and thus, the old nun began her tale:

My father's name was Yamada Kyoreki. He served Sir Ishida Jibusho Mitsunari in Hikone, which was in the Omi domain. Later, the above lord Jibusho rose in revolt against the Tokagawa clan and was blockaded at Ogaki Castle which is in the domain of Mino. Here at this siege is where we were all gathered together, myself included. While we were there, we had a bizarre experience in the castle, this is that story.

Every night around midnight, we heard voices of about thirty people, voices of men and women who we did not know, they called out 'Mr Tanaka Hyobu, Mr Tanaka Hyobu'. This was then followed by the sound of crying out. This was a weird thing and very fearful!

Later, the massive army of Lord Ieyasu closed in on us and there we were assaulted day and night. This force against us was led by Tanaka Hyobu. When we were going to fire a stone cannonball at his force from the inside of our castle, the men announced that they were about to do so, shouting it here and there.

'Why was that?' asked the children.

They told us this because when a stone was shot, the towers of our castle were shaken so tremendously that it felt as if the ground would split and weak-kneed women often fainted at this, it was a hard time. That is why they went around warning us all. Whenever we heard that, it felt like waiting for thunder after seeing lightning. At the beginning, we thought we were going to die and we could not think of anything, nothing came to us apart from fear. However, afterwards we did not care for it very much any more, as we were used to it. My mother and the other wives and daughters were all in the castle tower, casting bullets. As well as this, the severed enemy heads taken by our allies were gathered in the tower so that we could put name tags onto them, we did this so that we remembered who they were. We would also blacken the teeth in the head.

'Why was that?' asked the children.

It is because those heads with blackened teeth were considered to be decent warriors. Therefore, we were told to apply the colour to those heads with white teeth. Remember, heads are not what you should be afraid of, back then we even slept among the heads with the smell of blood in the air. (See Fig 21)

One day we were attacked with muskets by the besiegers and all people within the castle fell into fear and confusion, more than normal, this was because the castle appeared to be falling to the enemy that day. A high-ranking retainer came to us and said, 'The enemy is out of sight now. Do not fuss yourselves any more and calm down, just, calm down.' Just then a bullet flew in and hit my 14-year-old brother. He fell into a spasm and died. I must say, the scene I saw then was really tragic.

On that day, a Yabumi letter tied to an arrow flew into where my father was positioned in the castle, and it said 'Kyoreki, a teacher to Lord Ieyasu has spoken up for you as he has a connection to you and reason to speak on your behalf, thus, if you want to escape from the castle, your life will be spared. You may flee to any province you like. All troops have been instructed to let you go. Therefore, you will not have trouble on your way out.' Since being told the castle would fall the next day, we all had lost heart and feared that we might be killed on the morrow. My father secretly came over to the castle tower and told my mother and us to follow him. He then took us and put a ladder down from the side of the north wall attached to a rope. We went from here and we crossed over the moat in a wooden washtub. (See Fig 22)

Our party consisted of my parents, myself and a senior retainer, four in all and we left all the other retainers behind.

When we had gone as far as 5 or 6 cho north from the castle, my mother suddenly had pains in her stomach and delivered a baby girl. One retainer bathed her in the water of a rice field, and covered her with the skirt of his kimono. My father took my mother on his shoulder and we all made for the direction of Aonogahara. How fearful this experience was. Alas the old days, Nanmaida, Nanmaida.[2] (See Fig 23)

When the children asked the old nun again, 'please tell us about Hikone' – she told the following tale:

My father was given a fief of 300 koku, but there were so many battles at that time and we had a very difficult time with everything.

Though we all had little savings, what we had every morning and evening was porridge, this we ate almost every day. Sometimes my brother went hunting with his musket in the mountains, then we

---

2   A Buddhist prayer

cooked rice with greens and he took it as his lunch. When he ventured on these hunting excursions, we also got to eat this meal, so I often asked him to go hunting and if he did I became happy and excited.

Also we did not have enough clothes, I had nothing else but one summer kimono dyed pale blue that was handmade for me at the age of 13. As I was wearing the same thing until I was 17, it was too short for me and it did not even cover my shins, which was a great nuisance. All I wished for was to have a Katabira gown that would cover my shins. As you see from this, we had a very difficult life at that time. We could not eat lunch at all, nor take any late night meals. Young people these days care too much about clothes and are so obsessed with it that they spend money, or complain about food. It is so absurd.

[Commentary by a family member]:

She would always tell the children off by bringing up this old story of Hikone, and because of this, the children ended up calling her 'Hikone Baba' or the Hag of Hikone. Even now, we use the word 'talk about Hikone' to mean old people who criticise the current society by bringing up their past stories. It is said that the idiom originated from this old woman and it is only a local word and those from other provinces would not understand it.

Her father, Yamada Kyoreki, became a ronin and went down to Tosa, where he sought help from a relative, named Yamada Kisuke (who later became Yamada Youya). Oan married Amenomori Giemon, and after Giemon's death, she was supported by the above Yamada Kisuke. Oan was an aunt to Kisuke. She died at over 80 years old, which was during the Kanbun era of 1661-73.

I [the author and family member] was eight or nine years old when hearing the above old stories from her on occasions, which I have remembered since then. The saying that, 'time flies like an arrow' holds true indeed.

During the Shotoku Era of 1711 to 1715, I told this story to my grandchildren and criticised them, putting together all ancient things to show how much waste there is these days. However, the cheeky grandchildren said to me, 'The old woman was the Hikone Hag while you, our grandfather are a Hikone Jii, that is an old codger and that the world must change with time,' they think I am talking nonsense and they stick their noses up at me. It makes me angry, but all I can say is 'You should have fear about the future as you never know what will happen.' In turn, my grandchildren will be sniffed at by their grandchildren someday. There was nothing else to say so I just chanted a word of prayer, 'Mammaida, Mammaida'.

[Commentary by a later author]:

The above writing is an admirable and true story. Who recorded it is unknown. Possibly it was a memorandum by someone from the Yamada family. It was possessed by Tanaka Denzaemon and I borrowed it from him.

Kyoho 15 (1730) the Year of Kanoe Inu, the twenty-seventh day of the third month.

By Tanikakimori[3]

Okiku Monogatari
The Story of Okiku
(probably seventeenth century)

The grandmother of Tanaka Itoku – who was a doctor of the Ikeda clan – used to serve Yodo-dono[4] in Osaka and her name was Kiku.

On the day when Osaka Castle fell, which was 5 May 1615, she was in a Nagatsubone chamber which was a place for companion ladies. They were totally oblivious to the fall of the castle that day and she gave some buckwheat to a female servant and ordered her to make pancakes. Then the servant left for the kitchen. After that, she was informed that the area around the Tamatsukuriguchi exit had been burnt down, and some other areas were also engulfed in flames. Next she heard a great uproar and went out to the external corridor of the main hall, there she beheld the entire area in flames. Upon seeing this, she went back to the chamber, took out her summer kimono and put on three layers of dress. Also, she put on three pieces of underwear and put a mirror – given by Lord Hideyori – into her clothes and went out to the kitchen. There,

---

3   1698-1752, a Confucian and scholar of Japanese classics.
4   The concubine of Toyotomi Hideyoshi.

in the kitchen stood Takeda Eiou, wearing black armour, he had two unknown samurai with him at this time. One unknown samurai was asking a maidservant, outside of the kitchen, to take care of an injury to his shoulder and to tie his sash for him, but upon hearing his voice, the maid did not pay any attention to him and left the place in a rush. The warrior Takeda Eiou instructed us not to go out, but they did not care at all and left.

They found the Umajirushi standard of golden gourds left behind, and she, together with a servant named Oacha and one more, considered this to be shameful, so they broke the standard and threw it away. After that, they finally got out of the castle, there were the shield walls of bamboo but no warriors, neither inside nor outside of the castle, not even a wounded man could be seen. After a while, a man in a summer kimono came out from behind the bamboo shields, drawing a rusty sword and told them to give him any money that they had. She gave him two ingots and asked him which way General Todo was forming his defence. He replied that it was at the Matsubaraguchi exit, upon hearing this they asked him to take them there, and said if he did, they would give him more money. Thus he led them saying, 'Come this way.' On their way, they saw Yokoin-dono[5] (who was a high-ranking lady) who was being carried on the back of a samurai with another samurai helping them by supporting her feet as they escaped. The party also had other samurai and maidservants following them. On seeing them, they immediately rushed up to them and joined their escape. The party dropped by a house in Moriguchi, where we laid down straw mats and two old Tatami mats. They placed Yokoin-dono on two Tatami mats and we ourselves sat on the straw ones. They had a wooden half-barrel of steamed rice, the rice was served on paper and we all ate it.

She did not know where they got that rice from, but this was probably given by Wakasa-no-Kami because Yokoin-dono was only staying in the castle for the negotiation of a possible reconciliation, the fall of the castle just happened to take place during her stay there. (See Fig 24)

One of the attendants was a daughter of Yamashiro Kunai, who was serving Lord Hideyori, and she was wearing only one katabira and one

---

5   A sister of Yodo-dono (on the side of the castle) and mother of Kyogoku Wakasa-no-Kami (who was on the besieging side), she was in the castle trying to negotiate, and she had been caught inside the castle.

piece of underwear. As Kiku felt sorry for her, she took off one layer of her katabira and underwear and gave them to the woman.

In the meantime, Yokoin-dono was summoned by Lord Ieyasu and a palanquin came for her. Before leaving, the lady said to the attendants, 'though you are women, you were in the castle and I have no idea what Lord Ieyasu's orders will be and any order could be given. However, I will speak for you as well as I can but still you will have to follow whatever he orders, be well prepared for what is to come.' With these words, everyone grieved deeply. After a while she returned and as soon as she got off the palanquin, she told them that the lord would allow everyone to go wherever they liked and have someone see us safely away. At this news we could not be happier. Then Kiku hoped to visit Matsunomaru-dono in Kyoto, but Kunai's daughter, who was also among them, did not know where to go and asked me to let her accompany me. On their way to Kyoto, they dropped in on a merchant, who lived in Osaka. Though they did not think much of him when they were within the castle, he was better off than we expected. However, as they were refugees from Osaka Castle, it was inappropriate for him to let them stay even for one night, so he gave them each a roll of cloth instead. Next, they went to Oda Samon-dono's mansion, but they could not gain entry. However, Kunai's daughter, who was still with me at this point, was actually Samon-dono's niece and she told them she was with us and asked why they would not permit us to enter. Upon this information, we were taken in immediately and treated much better than was to be expected. Samon-dono showed us courtesy, thinking he could save his niece thanks to her efforts. While staying at the Samon-dono residence for four or five days, they had to stay on the second storey, which was not so lavish, and also they had to take meals there too. Therefore, she took her leave and headed for Matsunomaru-dono's residence. When she left, Samon-dono unexpectedly gave her a Katabira robe and five silver coins. In the end Kiku ended up serving Matsunomaru-dono[6] and later on got married to Itoku's grandfather and ended up in Bizen and died there.

It was not known what happened to the servant who was ordered to make the buckwheat pancake. People said that Lord Hideyori, Yodo-dono, Okura-kyo and all the other major people had moved into the

---

6   A mistress of Lord Hideyoshi.

Yamazato[7] tea rooms as early as two or three days before the fall of the castle, so none of them were in the castle tower at the break of the siege. Whether they were dead or not is unknown. (See Fig 25)

Extra information on the castle siege by the original chronicler:

Before the fall of the castle, a bullet came from nowhere and went through a maid and smacked into the side of the cupboard. It is said the edge of a Tatami mat was torn off as the bullet went past. It was also said the bullet weighed 30 momme and when it was weighed in hand, this seemed to be correct. After this event, they hung a curtain in the direction from where it came.

War councils were always had in the same chamber and were held in the deepest part of the quarters, therefore the above Okiku had had a chance to overhear them.

In the castle, they would pound and make Mochi rice cakes almost every day. This Mochi was delivered to each chamber, where one piece was left in front of each samurai in the early morning. As it was that often, people tended not to appreciate it and sometimes left it as it was. In such a case, the deliverer put the one of the previous day against the wall, and added a new one each day.

Okiku saw the coming of age ceremony of Obinsobi[8] for the girl Tenjuin-sama[9], when she was standing on the Go board, Lord Hideyori cut a bit of her hair with a short sword.

The meals for Yodo-dono were prepared by the staff in the kitchen and passed to the serving attendants. The servants in the kitchen tasted it for poison before they passed it to the attendants. Or sometimes the attendants tasted before they offered it to the lady.

Before the fall of the castle, a monk of the Tofukuji temple of Kyoto, whose name was the reverend Gesshin, had been staying in the castle. Kiku asked him, 'We will take leave and go up to Kyoto soon, until then could you keep this box for me? If I die within the castle, would you please perform a memorial service for us?' Then she put some clothes

---

7   A facility built for the tea ceremony within the castle.
8   A coming-of-age ceremony for females, performed at the age of 16. Her fiancée, father or brother should cut a small amount of her hair from the side of her head.
9   Lord Hideyori's wife, a daughter of Lord Ieyasu.

and vessels in a box and gave it to Gesshin. Some of the contents are still kept within the Tanaka family.

Kiku served Yodo-dono because Kiku's father, Yamaguchi Mozaemon was a son of Yamaguchi Mosuke and he was serving Azai Nagamasa. Yodo-dono – who Kiku was serving – was a daughter of Nagamasa and Kiku had served her since she was very young. Mozaemon later was employed by Todo Izumi-no-kami Takatora for a 300 koku income as a paid guest. However, as he heard about the Siege of Osaka, he decided to volunteer to work for the castle's forces, which was accepted, and he was given armour right away. However, he was killed in battle and it is unknown what exactly happened to him in the end. However, he was given armour, but as he did not have a standard or banner, he asked his daughter, Kiku, to make one for him. She sewed red and white silk together to make a standard. With this, he was very pleased and thanked her very much for her help – which must have been his way of saying goodbye. The reason he was employed by Todo is this: Todo Takatora used to be an ashigaru foot soldier serving the Asai clan – when he had the name of Yoemon – and Mosuke, the father of Mozaemon – who was Kiku's grandfather – was his sergeant. At that time Todo Takatora was so poor that he could not have breakfast at times, and Mosuke's wife – Kiku's grandmother – felt sorry for him and treated him with a simple meal from time to time. Feeling obliged to Mosuke's wife for the kindness, Todo Takatora invited Mozaemon – Kiku's father – and offered him a position as a paid guest. Mosuke ended up being paid up to 1,200 koku while serving the Asai clan.[10]

This is the end of the tales of females in Japanese warfare.

---

10 A small section of writing has been deleted here. It was a commentary by a later author and is an opinion on the story. The commentary is uninformative and has therefore been taken out.

Samurai Tales – A Brief Overview of the Samurai Found Within

The following is information about and outlines of the samurai found within the Musha Monogatari or samurai tales scroll. The articles they feature in are alongside their names and a basic selection of information concerning their life has been given.

Abiko Sakudayu – Article 30
Unknown date; a retainer to Niwa Nagashige.

Akai Akuemon – Article 26
1529–1578; his original name was Akai Naomasa, known to be intrepid and commonly known as Akuemon, 'evil one', and his nickname was the red devil (oni) of Tanba. He came from the Akai Family of Tanba province and was the second adopted son and husband to the daughter of Ogino Iyo-no-kami, a castle lord, but he later killed his father-in-law, and took the castle. He then led the Akai family and reconciled with Oda Nobunaga and gained three districts. He died from disease.

Akashi Kamon-no-suke Takenori – Article 56
Unknown dates; a general and tactician serving Ukiga Hideie, who was a Sengoku daimyo with a fief of 550,000 koku. In the Musha Monogatari, it is said he was killed in the Summer Siege of Osaka Castle but according to one theory, he was missing and actually fled.

Akechi Hyuga-no-kami Mitsuhide – Articles 5, 26 and 40
*c.*1528–1582; served Oda Nobunaga and destroyed him in the Honnoji
Incident in 1582, betraying him and forcing his suicide. Not much
is known about his early days. First he was a ronin and then served the
Asakura clan, then the Ashikaga shogun and finally Oda Nobunaga. He is
said to have been very smart, capable and good at tactics. Promoted highly
by Nobunaga and given 300,000 to 500,000 koku before the Honnoji
Incident. However, Nobunaga is said to have treated his retainers very
harshly and that Mitsuhide had a grudge against Nobunaga. After the
Honnoji Incident, Mitsuhide was defeated by Toyotomi Hideyoshi, who
unexpectedly came back to Kyoto to confront him, destroying this highly
ambitious samurai's lust to rule Japan. Eventually he was killed by a peasant
while running away from the battle with Hideyoshi.

Amakasu (Kagemochi) Omi-no-kami – Article 22
?–1604; one of the best retainers to Uesugi Kenshin and famous for his
bravery, he moved to Yonezawa, accompanying the Lord of the Uesugi
clan and died there of natural causes.

Amago Haruhisa – Article 41
1514–1561; the grandson of Amago Tsunehisa – who was the Shugo
daimyo of Izumo province – Haruhisa led this influential family from the
age of 23. He competed with the Ouchi clan for a prolonged period but
he died suddenly at the age of 47.

Amago Katsuhisa – Article 41
1553–1578; After the Amago family was ruined by Mouri Motonari in
1568, the retainers tried to restore the clan by helping Katsuhisa retake the
clan. They were defeated by Mouri and their attempt failed. Therefore,
they served under Oda Nobunaga's control and as part of Hideyoshi's
campaign over west Honshu, when Amago took Kozuki Castle against
the Mouri clan. However, Oda's support collapsed and the castle
surrendered in the end. Amago killed himself at the age of 26 after the
surrender.

Ando Chosaburo – Articles 35 and 56
Unknown dates; a retainer of Ii Naotaka. Due to him taking the head of
Kimura Nagato-no-kami, he was a given 500 koku salary, however, he

was not happy with this amount and left the Ii clan and consulted with an influential relative, Ando Tatewaki. Tatewaki in anger forced the Ii clan to rehire Chosaburo at the salary of 1,000 koku.

Ando Tatewaki – Article 56

1555–1635; a close retainer of Tokugawa Ieyasu, trusted by Ieyasu so much so that he was assigned as a senior counsellor of Kishu in 1610 with a 38,000 koku salary. He died of natural causes.

Asahina Sozaemon – Article 56

Unknown dates; was a retainer to Imagawa Ujizane.

Asai Kii-no-kami Yoshinaga – Article 61

1576–1613; retainer of Toyotomi Hideyoshi, his father was Hideyoshi's brother-in-law. Took the East side (Ieyasu side) in the Battle of Sekigahara and after the victory was given 378,000 koku of Kishu domain and died in Wakayama from disease. The family then moved, in the early seventeenth century, to Hiroshima Domain.

Ashikaga Takauji – Article 21

1305–1358; he was a vassal of the Kamakura shogunate and ordered to gain supremacy over the Emperor Godaigo, who had raised an army against the shogunate with the help of Kusunoki Masashige. Takauji settled this dispute, however, two years later, he decided to take sides with the Emperor Godaigo and drove the shogunate to collapse in 1333. However, the restoration to full power made by the Emperor Godaigo totally failed and Takauji raised an army against the emperor and founded the Ashikaga shogunate in 1338.

Ashina Yoshihiro (also: Morishige) – Article 48

1575–1631; second son of Satake Yoshishige, who was a very powerful daimyo in north Honshu. Adopted by and inherited the Ashina clan, which was also a very powerful daimyo family, at the age of 12. He was defeated by Date Masamune in the Battle of Suriagehara and fled home, to Satake. His land was confiscated by Hideyoshi but later 16,000 koku was given back in the Edo period. He died from disease at the age of 57.

Atsumi Gengo – Article 47
Unknown dates; a retainer to Tokugawa Ieyasu, he features in a poem alongside Hattori Hanzo and Watanabe Hanzo as a great retainer, his nickname was 'Headhunter Gengo'.

Baba Mino-no-kami Nobufusa – Article 56
1514–1575; one of the twenty-four generals for Takeda Shingen and served the Takeda clan for more than forty years. He fought more than seventy battles and is said to have never received a single injury.

Ban Dan'emon Naoyuki – Articles 56 and 60
1567–1615; retainer of Kato Yoshiaki. In the Korean Campaigns, he performed great deeds and for this was assigned as the head of 200 musketeers at the Battle of Sekigahara. However, when the battle began, he himself charged into the enemy with a spear, leaving his men behind. He was accused of this misdeed later and left the clan. He served various different lords but it did not work because of his former lord's intervening in the matter. He joined the Osaka side in the famous sieges and was killed in the Summer Siege of 1615.

Cho Kurozaemon-no-jo Tsuratatsu – Article 30
1546–1619; he was from the Cho clan who served the Hatakeyama clan in Noto. In 1577, his family were all killed by Yusa Tsugumitsu and Nukui Kagetora, who were also retainers of the Hatakeyama and only Tsuratatsu survived. He moved to serve Oda Nobunaga and after years of fighting both Yusa and Nukuui, he finally succeeded in killing Yusa Tsugumitsu and his son in 1581. After Nobunaga's death he became a key vassal of the Maeda clan of Kaga province.

Date Awa-no-kami Shigezane – Article 48
1568–1646; cousin and retainer of Date Masamune, given approximately a 38,000 koku salary by Masamune, but left the clan for some reason unknown. Returned to the clan five years later and served as a senior councillor under Masamune's son. Died in 1646 of natural causes.

Date Masamune – Articles 21, 34, 48 and 52
1567–1636; a Sengoku period daimyo of the Dewa and Mutsu provinces. Through battles against those clans in north Honshu, he took hold of the entire area. He barely survived conflicts with Hideyoshi and Ieyasu, and

became the first lord of Sendai province, which was the third biggest economic power at that time. Died from disease at the age of 70. He liked gorgeous and magnificent clothing so 'Date' came to mean 'fashionable'. Darth Vader's mask was allegedly created based on images of this helmet.

Date Terumune – Article 34
1544–1585; father of the above Date Masamune, according to the story, he was killed by his son or his son's troops as they tried to rescue him from Nihonmatsu, who had kidnapped him in 1585.

Echizen Shosho Tadanao – Article 14
1595–1650; his father, Yuki Hideyasu, was the second son of Tokugawa Ieyasu. He was the daimyo of Fukui.

Eguchi Saburozaemon – Article 8
Unknown dates; a retainer of Niwa Nagashige of Kaga province, he later served Yuki Hideyasu with the fief of 10,000 koku.

Fukushima Saemon-dayu Masanori – Article 17, 39 and 55
1561–1624; retainer of Toyotomi Hideyoshi, then Tokugawa Ieyasu and Okugawa Hidetada. Given a very high fief and position by Hideyoshi, but after the latter's death, and due to the conflicts with Ishida Mitsunari, he took the Tokugawa side. Because of his great feats in the Battle of Sekigahara, he was given 490,000 koku. However, in 1619 he was punished for his infringement of the laws (which may have been a political issue) and deprived of most of his fief.

Fukushima Tanba-no-kami Harushige – Article 39
1557–1630; a retainer to the Fukushima clan and on a salary of 30,000 koku, he became a ronin after Fukushima Masanori lost his position, and died in Kyoto.

Fuwa Mokubei – Article 30
?–1600; retainer of Niwa Nagashige, died in the Battle of Asai Nawate.

Gamo Shimotsukeno-kami Tadasato – Article 37
1602–1628; grandson to Gamo Ujisato, he inherited Aizu province of 600,000 koku at the age of 10 but died from smallpox at the age of 26.

Gamo Ujisato – Articles 17 and 45
1556–1595; a retainer of Oda Nobunaga and afterwards, of Toyotomi Hideyoshi. He was Nobunaga's son-in-law and was given Aizu province of 420,000 koku by Hideyoshi. He died from disease at the age of 40.

Genzanmi (also, Minamoto-no) Nyudo Yorimasa – Article 2
1104–1180; he was the primary warrior of the Minamoto clan. After decades of clashes between Minamoto and the Taira clans, Yorimasa raised an army and defended Byodoin temple. He killed himself at Byodoin and legend says that his retainers took his head away so that the enemy could not get it. He was also famous as an excellent poet.

Goto Matabei Mototsugu – Article 35
1560–1615; retainer of Kuroda Yoshitaka. After Yoshitaka's death, he left the Kuroda clan due to the conflicts with Yoshitaka's son. Though he had several offers to serve powerful daimyo, he became ronin because of interference from Yoshitaka's son. At the Sieges of Osaka, he joined the Toyotomi side and was killed in 1615.

Hachisuka Awa-no-kami – Articles Yoshishige 46 and 60
1586–1620; served Toyotomi Hideyoshi but at the Battle of Sekigahara, took the side of Tokugawa. Given 257,000 koku as an income but died from disease at the age of 35.

Haiga Jidayu – Article 30
Unknown dates; a retainer to Niwa Nagashige, he died in the Battle of Asai Nawate.

Hajikano Den'emon – Article 7
1545–1624; a retainer of the Takeda clan, after the Takeda clan was ruined he served the Tokugawa clan and died from disease.

Haneda Inaba-no-kami – Article 48
Unknown dates; a retainer to the Date clan.

Hattori Den'emon – Article 37 and 56
Unknown dates; no information is known on him bar the articles in this book.

Hattori Hanzo – Article 47
1542–1597; born in Mikawa province from an Iga background he served Tokugawa Ieyasu and was one of the sixteen Great Generals. Known as Devil Hanzo apparently for his outstanding tactics in warfare. He was awarded a spear for his battle achievements and led a force of 200 Iga-no-Mono (ninja) under the Tokugawa clan. Hanzomon, 'the gate of Hanzo' – a principle gate in Edo Castle – is named after him, as is the modern train line. He appears in the poem with 'Spear Hanzo' and 'Head-Taker Gengo'.

Hojo Ujimasa – Articles 21 and 60
1538–1590; the fourth inheritor of the Go-Hojo clan, a Sengoku family in Kanto district. Together with Ujiyasu, his father, their territory became the largest in the clan's history and approximated to 2,400,000 koku during the period of his lordship; but in 1590, at the Siege of Odawara by Toyotomi Hideyoshi, after months of defending Odawara Castle, he surrendered and killed himself.

Hojo Ujiyasu – Articles 15, 21, 25 and 60
1515-1571; the third inheritor of the Go-Hojo clan. While achieving a triple alliance with the Takeda and Imagawa clans, he successfully expanded his territory through battles against the Uesugi, Ashikaga and other clans. He died from disease at the age of 57.

Hojo Saemon-dayu Tsunashige – Article 15
1515–1587; a retainer of the Go-Hojo clan and son-in-law to Hojo Ujitsuna. On the night of the Battle of Kawagoe, a famous Go-Hojo victory, he achieved the greatest feat and was given Kawagoe Castle. He became a monk after Ujiyasu died in 1571.

Hojo Tango-no-kami Kagehiro – Article 56
1548–1579; a retainer to Uesugi Kenshin. In the war of Odate, which took place over the succession to the family headship after the death of Kenshin, he fought for Uesugi Kagetori and was killed by Ogino Shume.

Honda Hachizo Shigetsugu – Article 56
1529–1596; a retainer to the Tokugawa clan, he was famous for his great feats in battle and ability in the political arena. He died from disease at the age of 68.

Honda Heihachiro Tadakatsu – Article 10
1548–1610; a retainer of Tokugawa Ieyasu, given 100,000 koku as salary, the second largest given to one of Ieyasu's direct retainers. He died from disease at the age of 63.

Honda Sanya Masashige – Article 42
1545–1617; a retainer of the Tokugawa clan but left their service in 1575 and served Takigawa Kazumasa, Maeda Toshiie and Gamo Ujisato, but went back to Tokugawa in 1596. He became a daimyo and was given 10,000 koku and died at the age of 73.

Horio Tatewaki Yoshiharu – Article 50
1544–1611; used to be a close retainer of Toyotomi Hideyoshi but took the side of Tokugawa at the Battle of Sekigahara. He died at the age of 68.

Ikeda Musashi-no-kami Terunao – Article 11
1584–1616; the second inheritor of the Ikeda clan, which was a powerful daimyo family in Okayama. He died at the age of 33 – a popular belief says he was poisoned by his stepmother.

Ibano Todayu – Article 11
Unknown dates; a retainer to Ikeda Terunao, he was famous for his mastery in archery.

Ii Kamon-no-kami Naotaka – Article 35
1590–1659; a retainer to Tokugawa Ieyasu and Tokugawa Hidetada. He was the second daimyo of Hikone province and died at the age of 70.

Ikeda Shokuro Motosuke – Article 56
c.1559–1584; son of Ikeda Tsuneoki and first retainer of Oda Nobunaga. After Nobunaga's death, he became a retainer of Toyotomi Hideyoshi. When his father was given Ogaki Castle in Mino province, he also was assigned as lord of Gifu Castle. They were both killed at the Battle of Nagakute.

Ikeda Shonyu Tsuneoki – Article 56
1536–1584; a retainer to Oda Nobunaga. After the death of Nobunaga, took sides with Hideyoshi. He was killed in the Battle of Nagakute against Tokugawa Ieyasu.

Imagawa Ujizane – Article 21
1538–1614; a Sengoku period daimyo of Suruga, Mikawa and Totoumi provinces. After his father was killed by Oda Nobunaga at the Battle of Okehazama, his territory grew smaller and smaller, and was attacked by Tokugawa Ieyasu and thus surrendered. Given refuge and harboured by the Go-Hojo and Tokugawa until he died in 1614.

Imagawa Yoshimoto – Articles 56 and 57
1519–1560; father to the above and a Sengoku period daimyo of Suruga, Mikawa, Totoumi provinces. He was killed in the Battle of Okehazama. The Imagawa clan was ruined 9 years after this battle.

Inawashiro Moritane – Article 48
Unknown dates; a retainer of the Ashina clan.

Inoue Kanzaemon – Article 30
Unknown dates; a retainer to Ota Tajima-no-Kami.

Inoue Kurozaemon Yukifusa – Article 23
1554–1634; a chief vassal of the Kuroda clan, he was to serve over four generations of the lord's family.

Ishida Jibunosho Mitsunari – Articles 20, 30 and 50
1560–1600; a retainer of Toyotomi Hideyoshi and Hideyori. After the death of Hideyoshi, he confronted the then renegade Tokugawa Ieyasu and fought with him at the Battle of Sekigahara, splitting the country in half. He was defeated and captured alive, displayed in public and decapitated in Kyoto.

Iwata Denzaemon – Article 30
Unknown dates; a retainer to Ota Tajima-no-kami.

Izutsu On'na-no-suke – Article 16
Unknown dates; all that is known about him appears in Article 16.

Kaganoe Yahachiro – Article 50
1561–1600; a retainer of Toyotomi Hideyoshi and lord of Kaganoi Castle in Mino with 10,000 koku. He attacked Horie Yoshiharu and Mizuno Tadashige and was killed by Horie.

Kakizaki Izumi-no-kami – Kageie Article 22
?–1575; a close retainer of Uesugi Kenshin. Due to a suspicion that he was communicating secretly with Oda Nobunaga, he was killed by order of Kenshin.

Kanazawa Bicchu Tanemasa – Article 43
Unknown dates; father of Kanazawa Chubyoe, a retainer of Souma Yoshitane.

Kanazawa Chubyoe Masao – Article 43
?–1635; a close retainer of Souma Yoshitane. When his lord Yoshitane died, he killed himself to follow his lord to the grave and was buried alongside him.

Katakura Kojuro – Article 48
1557–1615; close retainer and tactician of Date Masamune, died from disease at the age of 59.

Kato Akinari – Article 53
1592–1661; son of Kato Sama-no-suke Yoshiaki, he inherited Aizu province which was worth 400,000 koku. Greedy and cruel as a person, in 1639 an incident took place where a senior councillor, Hori Mondo, left the clan and attacked positions as he left, firing muskets at the castle and breaking through checkpoints. Akinari sent off pursuers and from there Hori went up to Mt Koya and sent a petition asking the shogun for help. As a result, Hori Mondo was handed over to Akinari, and he was executed by being buried up to his neck while people sawed at his neck with a bamboo saw. This was followed by lots of criticism and the shogunate deprived him of his fief, with a 10,000 koku income saved for his son, which was issued in 1643. Akinari retired then and in 1661 he died at the age of 69.

Kato Sama-no-suke Yoshiakira – Articles 37 and 53
1563–1631; a retainer of Toyotomi Hideyoshi. After Hideyoshi's death, he took the side of Tokugawa Ieyasu.

Kawada Hachisuke – Article 4
?–1626; a retainer of Kobayakawa Takakage.

Kawai Sanjuro – Article 56
Unknown dates; a retainer of Ban Naomasa.

Kawajiri Yohyoe Hidetaka – Article 56
1527–1582; a retainer to the Oda clan. After the Incident of Honnoji, where Nobunaga died, he did not withdraw from Koshu – like other retainers – in an attempt to keep the territory, but he ended up being killed in a riot.

Kawamura Shinpachiro – Articles 46 and 56
Unknown date; a retainer of Mizuno Katsunari.

Kawagi Gorozaemon – Article 53
Unknown dates; a retainer of Kato Yoshiaki.

Kawaya Shinzaemon – Article 56
Unknown dates; a retainer of Mouri Terumoto.

Kimura Nagato-no-kami Shigenari – Articles 35 and 56
?–1615; a retainer to Toyotomi Hideyori. Shigenari's mother was Hideyori's nursemaid and he served Hideyori from a very young age. When he was killed in the Summer Siege of Osaka in 1615, his wife, whom he had been married to for five months, was pregnant and she became a nun after she delivered a son. She killed herself after she held the one-year anniversary of her husband's death.

Komeda Kenmotsu – Article 61
Unknown dates; a retainer of the Hosokawa clan. At the Summer Siege of Osaka Castle, he joined the Toyotomi side together with his lord, Hosokawa Okiaki, while Okiaki's father, Tadaoki, fought for the Tokugawa side. After the siege, Tadaoki ordered Okiaki – the lord – to kill himself but Komeda was allowed to come back to serve the Hosokawa clan as a senior councillor at a later date.

Konishi Manbei – Article 26
?–1579; a retainer of Akechi Mitsuhide.

Kozukuri Taizen Tomoyasu – Article 38
Unknown dates; he served Oda Nobukatsu and then Oda Hidenobu.
At the Battle of Sekigahara he advised Hidenobu to take sides with
Tokugawa, but Hidenobu would not listen to him and went to the West
side and they were annihilated. Afterwards, he went into service for
Fukushima Masanori at a salary of 20,000 koku.

Kuroda Josui Nyudo Masanari – Article 23
1546–1604; close retainer of Toyotomi Hideyoshi, he, together with
Takenaka Shigeharu (Hanbei), were said to be the best strategists under
Hideyoshi. He first served Kodera Masamoto as a senior councillor
but thought much of Oda Nobunaga's talents and advised his lord to
approach Nobunaga. When his lord intended to support Araki Murashige,
who rebelled against Nobunaga, Kuroda Masanari went to Murashige's
castle to persuade him to surrender but was captured and imprisoned in
the castle for one year. However, as he did not come back immediately,
Nobunaga thought Masanari had betrayed him and ordered his son to be
killed. However, Takenaka Hanbei sheltered his son and had Hideyoshi
(Nobugaga's son) present a false (or rather a substitute) head in place of
the boy's. One year later, when the castle was captured, Masanari was
saved and thanked Hanbei deeply for what he did and took Takenaka's
family crest as his own. He served Nobunaga and Hideyoshi with his
gifted strategies and after Nobunaga's death, he served as a close associate
of Hideyoshi and was rewarded with a fief of 120,000 koku in Buzen.

Kurokawa Kahyoe – Article 53
Unknown dates; a retainer of Kato Yoshiaki.

Maeda Magoshiro Hizen-no-kami Toshikatsu (also Toshinaga) – Article 30
1562–1614; the son and heir to Maeda Toshiie, who was the most important associate of Toyotomi Hideyoshi and the founder of Kaga province.
After Hideyoshi and his father's death, he was expected to lead the anti-
Tokugawa forces, but chose to take sides with Tokugawa Ieyasu. After
the Battle of Sekigahara, because of his devotion, he was given extra fief
from Tokugawa Ieyasu, which added up to 1,020,000 koku. He died at
the age of 53 from disease, however the Kaikei Yawa document says he
killed himself by taking poison to solve the conflicts between his family
and the shogun.

Machino Nagato-no-kami Yukikazu – Article 37
?–1647; he served Gamo Ujisato, and was the lord of Nihonmatsu Castle. He moved to Shirakawa accompanying Ujisato, who was transferred there. Later he was expelled from the clan due to some dispute with a colleague and became ronin and was subsequently hired by the shogunate as the captain of musketeers with a fief of 5,000 koku.

Maeda Matazaemonnojo Toshiie – Article 50
1539–1599; he started his service for Oda Nobunaga as a page and records[1] say he was a sexual partner to Nobunaga when he was young. He was in the Aka Horo Shu, or Red Cape Unit, in Nobunaga's bodyguards but had a fight with Nobunaga's half-brother and killed him. As a result Nobunaga suspended him from service. During the two years while he was suspended, he joined two battles without permission and succeeded to get three and two heads respectively. After the second battle, Nobunaga allowed him to come back to service. He was assigned to conquer the Hokuriku area under Shibata Katsuie's command and given Noto province with a fief of 230,000 koku by Nobunaga in 1581. After Nobunaga was killed in 1582, he was politically sandwiched between Hideyoshi and Shibata Katsuie and in the battle Shizugatake, Toshiie was at first under Katsuie's command but suddenly retreated, which made Hideyoshi the victor. He was appointed as the head of the council of Five Elders by Hideyoshi, so he would serve as a guardian for Hideyoshi's young son after his death, but Toshiie died one year after Hideyoshi did.

Matsudaira Genzaburo – Article 57
1554–1586; the half-brother of Tokugawa Ieyasu by a different father and taken in to the Imagawa clan as a hostage at a very young age but he escaped. Two years after, in 1568, he was delivered to the Takeda clan which is the story repeated in Article 57 of this book. When he escaped Koshu he did so in severe cold and lost almost all of his toes from frostbite.

Matsudaira Kyubei – Article 30
Unknown dates; a retainer of Maeda Toshinaga.

---

[1]   The document is titled 亜相公御夜話, but its provenance is unknown.

Matsuda Kinshiro Hidenobu – Article 45
?–1600; a retainer of Gamo Ujisato killed in the Battle of Sekigahara.

Matsuda Rokurozaemon-no-jo Sadakatsu – Article 25
Unknown dates; a retainer of Hojo Ujiyasu but later served Tokugawa
Hidetada.

Matsukura Ukon-no-dayu Shigenobu – Article 3
?–1593; a general in Tsutsui Junkei's army. He lived in Yamato province with a
fief of 2,500 koku, then transferred to Nabari of Iga with a fief of 8,300 koku.

Matsumura Magosaburo – Article 30
Unknown dates; a retainer to Niwa Nagashige.

Migiwa San'emon – Article 56
Unknown date; a retainer of Mizuno Katsunari.

Mii Yaichiro – Article 56
Unknown dates; all that is known about him is found in Article 56.

Mishuku Kanbei (Echizen-no-Kami) – Articles 14 and 56
?–1615; served Takeda Shingen and Katsuyori, then Hojo Ujinao. After the
Hojo clan was ruined, he was employed by Echizen-no-kami with a high
stipend of 10,000 koku. But after the lord's death, he fell into discord with
the lord's son and joined Osaka Castle and died in the Summer Siege of
1615.

Miura Yoji – Article 57
Unknown dates; a retainer to Imagawa Ujizane.

Mizukoshi Nui-no-suke – Article 30
Unknown dates; a retainer of Maeda Toshinaga.

Mizuno Hyuga-no-kami Katsunari – Article 46
1564–1651; starting with Oda Nobunaga, he successively served famous
warlords, including Toyotomi Hideyoshi, and went into service for the
Tokugawa clan at the end. Became the first daimyo of Fukuyama domain
and died at the age of 88.

Mizuno So-byoe-no-jo Tadashige – Article 50
1541–1600; lord of Kariya Castle of Mikawa. He served Oda Nobunaga, later Tokugawa Ieyasu. He was killed by Kaganoe Shigemasa just before the Battle of Sekigahara.

Mouri Motonari – Article 21, 27 and 41
1497–1571; called the 'supreme ruler' of Chugoku region and became valued as the most excellent of generals for generations. When he inherited the Mouri clan, the clan was only a small daimyo faction who had to pay attention to the wishes of other powerful daimyo. To start his rise he decided to oppose the Amago clan and took sides with the Ouchi clan. As well as fighting numerous battles, he increased his powerbase by sending his second son to the Kobayakawa clan and his third son to the Kikkawa clan to be adopted, who were both powerful clans. In 1562 Motonari defeated Sue at the Battle of Itsukushima with only one fifth the forces of those of the Sue army. He defeated the remnants of the Amago clan at the Battle of Gassan Toda Castle and got hold of eight provinces of the Chugoku region and became the most powerful daimyo in that area. He died from disease at the age of 75.

Mouri Shinsuke – Article 56
?–1582; a retainer of Oda Nobunaga. He killed Imagawa Yoshimoto at the Battle of Okehazama and at the time of the Incident of Honnoji, he was fighting for Oda Nobutada – Nobunaga's first son – but was killed in Nijo Castle.

Mori Shozo Nagayoshi – Article 56
1558–1584; a retainer of Oda Nobunaga and second son of Mori Yoshinari. He was also the elder brother of Mori Naritoshi. As his father and elder brother were killed in a battle in 1570, he inherited Kanayama Castle at the age of 13. After Nobunaga's death, he served Hideyoshi and was killed in the Battle of Nagakute after fighting fiercely.

Mori Ranmaru Naritoshi – Article 9
1565–1582; a retainer of Oda Nobunaga. A popular saying says he was also in a sexual relationship with Nobunaga. He was killed at the age of 18 in the Honnoji Incident together with Nobunaga himself.

Mukai Noto-no-kami – Article 58
Unknown dates; the only information for him is listed in Article 58.

Nagai Ukon Naokatsu – Article 56
1563–1625; a retainer of Tokugawa Ieyasu, he killed Ikeda Tsuneoki at
the Battle of Komaki Nagakute in 1584. Through fighting in the Siege
of Odawara, the Battle of Sekigahara, the Sieges of Osaka Castle and
elsewhere, he kept being promoted and ended as the first daimyo of Koga
domain with a fief of 72,000 koku. He died at the age of 63.

Nagao Hayato-no-suke Tanetsune (Kazukatsu) – Article 39
1550–1619; a retainer of Fukushima Masanori. He was one of three
Elders of the Fukushima clan. He was given a fief of 13,000 koku when
Masanori was given Aki province.

Nagaoka (also, Hosokawa) Yusai Fujitaka – Article 36
1534–1610; he served the thirteenth Ashikaga shogun, Yoshiteru and after
Yoshiteru's death, he gave support to the fifteenth shogun Yoshiaki. Later,
he went into the service of Oda Nobunaga and became a daimyo with a
fief of 150,000 koku in Tango province. He was a high-ranking retainer
of Hideyoshi and Ieyasu and was the founder of the Hosokawa clan
as daimyo of Higo domain. Also, he was considered a highly cultured
person, adept in various arts and he was especially famous as a poet.

Nagao Tamekage – Article 54
?–1536; a deputy of the Uesugi clan, which was the military governor
(shugo) in Echigo province. He died from disease.

Naito Shuri-no-suke Masatoyo – Article 56
1522–1575; a retainer of the Takeda clan. An excellent and most trusted
general of Takeda Shingen, killed in the Battle of Nagashino in 1575.

Nakagawa Sohan Mitsushige – Article 30
1562–1614; Maeda Toshiie's son in law and lord of Masuyam Castle in
Ecchu province.

Naeo Yamashiro-no-kami Kanetsugu – Article 22
1560–1619; a retainer of Uesugi Kagekatsu of Echigo province. When Kagekatsu was transferred to Aizu with a fief of 1,200,000 koku by Hideyoshi, Kanetsugu (the samurai of this article) was given 60,000 koku in Yonezawa province. After Hideyoshi's death, the Uesugi clan was attacked by Ieyasu in 1600 and surrendered. The Uesugi clan was again transferred to Yonezawa being curtailed to 300,000 koku. He died in Edo at the age of 60.

Narasaki Jubei – Article 4
Unknown dates; a retainer of Kobayakawa Takakage.

Narita Sukekuro – Article 30
Unknown dates; a retainer of Niwa Nagashige.

Natsuka Okura-no-tayu Masaie – Article 45
1562–1600; a retainer of Hideyoshi and one of the Five Commissioners of the Toyotomi administration. Lord of Minakuchi Castle with a fief of 120,000 koku. Defeated at the Battle of Sekigahara and killed himself at the age of 39.

Nihonmatsu Ukyo Yoshitsugu – Article 34
?–1585; lord of Nihonmatsu Castle, kidnapped Date Terumune and was killed by Terumune's son, Date Masamune, in 1585, as described in Article 34.

Nishio Nizaemon – Articles 14 and 56
Unknown dates; a retainer of Matsudaira Tadanao.

Niwa Gorozaemon Nagashige – Article 8 and 30
1535–1585; a retainer of Oda Nobunaga and given Wakasa province in 1573. After the Incident of Honnoji and together with Hideyoshi, he hunted down and killed Akechi Mitsuhide. After this, he was given the provinces Echizen, Wakasa and half of Kaga. He died from disease at the age of 51.

Nomoto Ukon – Articles 14 and 56
Unknown dates; a retainer to Matsudaira Tadanao of Echizen province.

Oda Hidenobu – Article 38
1580–1605; son of Oda Nobutada and grandson to Oda Nobunaga. Hideyoshi appointed him as inheritor of the Oda clan at the age of 3, but was considered Hideyoshi's puppet. At the Battle of Sekigahara, he joined the West side because he was invited to do so by Ishida Mitsunari, the commander of the West forces. He was fiercely attacked by Fukushima Masanori and surrendered. He became a monk and went to Mt Koya and died there at the age of 26.

Oda Nobunaga – Articles 9 and 57
1534–1582; born in Owari province he is one of Japan's most famous samurai, practically uniting the country. From a mid-level family, the Oda clan, he started a campaign of war, pitching the Sengoku period into its most bloodthirsty time. His story is exciting, long and complex. However, after all the long years at war against multiple factions, he was betrayed by Akechi Mitsuhide and he was caught by surprise in Honnoji temple, where he committed suicide in the burning temple; this is now known as the Honnoji Incident.

Oda Shichi-byoe Nobuzumi – Article 56
1555–1582; the nephew of Oda Nobunaga. Nobuzumi's father was Nobunaga's brother but was killed by Nobunaga on a charge of treason but Nobuzumi was raised by one of Nobunaga's close retainers and the boy served Nobunaga. Nobuzumi was married to a daughter of Akechi Mitsuhide – who orchestrated the death of Nobunaga. At the Honnoji Incident where Nobunaga died, Nobuzumi was killed due to an alleged suspicion of secret communications with Akechi Mitsuhide pertaining to this incident.

Ogasawara Kento – Article 8
Unknown dates; a retainer to Nisa Nagashige.

Ogita Shume Nagashige – Article 56
1562–1641; a retainer of the Uesugi clan. At the war of Odate, which was conducted over the succession to the leadership of the Uesugi clan, he took sides with Uesugi Kagekatsu and killed Kagekatsu's competitor, Uegusi Kagetora. After a period of being a ronin, he went into service for the Matsudaira clan of Echizen and, due to his achievements in the Sieges of Osaka Castle, he was given a fief of 25,000 koku.

Oka Chikuzen-no-kami – Article 41
Unknown dates; a retainer of Mouri Terumoto.

Ono Jin'nojo – Article 30
Unknown dates; a retainer of Ota Nagatomo.

Ono Shuri-no-suke – Article 46
?–1615; a close retainer of Hideyoshi and after Hideyoshi's death, he served his son Hideyori. He was killed in the Summer Siege of Osaka Castle as he attempted to follow Hideyori to the grave. There was a rumour that he had illicit relations with Yodo-dono (Hideyoshi's concubine) but there is no evidence for this.

Oroshi Hikozaemon – Articles 37 and 56
?–1582; a close retainer of Oda Nobunaga. He was killed in the Honnoji Incident.

Ota Dokan Mochisuke – Articles 1, 18 and 44
1432–1486; deputy to a Shugo governor of Musashi province and a senior councillor of the Ougiyatsu Uesugi clan. He built Edo Castle in 1457 – not the later one built by Tokugawa Ieyasu – and was assassinated on the order of Uesugi Sadamasa in 1486. He was also famous as a poet.

Otani Gyobu-no-sho Yoshitaka (also, Yoshitsugu) – Article 30
1559/65–1600; a close retainer of Toyotomi Hideyoshi, given a fief of 50,000 koku he became the lord of Tsuruga Castle in Echizen province. After Hideyoshi's death, he approached Tokugawa Ieyasu and he tried to persuade his close friend, Ishida Mitsunari, to follow Ieyasu. However, Ishida's resolution was so firm that Otani joined the West side at the Battle of Sekigahara, together with his three sons, for the sake of their friendship. In the battle, Yoshitaka's army was defeated owing to the betrayal of Kobayakawa Hideaki and so he killed himself at age of 42. His head was taken and buried by a retainer of his so that it could not be found by the enemy.

Ota Tajima-no-kami Nagatomo – Article 30
?–1602; a retainer of the Maeda clan and their premier senior. He was killed by the second senior councillor, Yokoyama Nagachika, by the order of Lord Maeda Toshinaga.

Otomo Shuri-no-tayu Yoshimune – Article 23
1558–1610; the twenty-second inheritor of the Otomo clan in Bungo province. After the Battle of Ishigakihara, he surrendered and was condemned to exile in Hitachi province. He died at the age of 53.

Ouchi Yoshitaka – Articles 12, 27 and 49
1507–1551; the thirty-first inheritor of the Ouchi clan, a powerful Sengoku daimyo in west Honshu. His close retainer, Sue Takafusa, rebelled against him, which resulted in Yoshitaka killing himself at the age of 45.

Ozeki Iwami-no-kami – Article 39
1571-1618; a chief retainer to Fukushima Masanori and given a fief of 20,000 koku.

Reizei Hangan Takatoyo – Article 27
1513–1551; a retainer to Ouchi Takafusa. He killed himself together with his lord, Yoshitaka, during the rebellion by Sue Takafusa.

Sakai Saemon-no-jo Tadatsugu – Article 57
1527–96; a chief retainer of Tokugawa Ieyasu, one of the Four Heavenly Kings of Tokugawa who were known as the Tokugawa Shitenno. The other three were Ii Naomasa, Honda Tadakatsu and Sakakibara Yasumasa.

Sanada Genjiro Nobutada – Article 15
1547–1632; Sanada Yukitaka's fourth son and uncle to Sanada Nobushige. A retainer of Tokugawa Ieyasu, he fought against his nephew Sanada Nobushige in the Battle of Sekigahara.

Sanada Saemon-no-suke Nobushige – Articles 14 and 56
1567–1615; commonly known as Sanada Yukimura. He was from the Sanada clan, who were a landlord and warrior family in Shinano province. His father, Sanada Masayuki, was Ashigaru Taisho or the foot-soldier commander, in Takeda Shingen's army. As Masayuki's elder brothers were killed at the Battle of Nagashino, he inherited the Sanada clan. After the Takeda clan was ruined and Oda Nobunaga died, the Sanada clan became independent and defended against Tokugawa's attack, where the Tokugawa side were repelled by Sanada's outstanding tactics. Nobushige

and his father fought for the West side and were defeated in the Battle of Sekigahara and after the war were deported to Kudoyama near Mt Koya – this punishment was asserted instead of seppuku (ritual suicide), due to the intervention of Nobushige's elder brother, Nobuyuki. His father, Masayuki, died while confined in Kudoyama. Just before the Winter Siege of Osaka Castle, Nobushige escaped from Kudoyama with his son and joined the Toyotomi army in the castle. Through the two sieges, his feats are considered the most impressive ones performed by those on the Toyotomi side, especially in the Summer Siege, where he directly attacked Ieyasu's headquarters, which endangered Ieyasu. Soon after this attack, while treating injured men, he was killed and decapitated.

Sasa-no-Saizo – his correct name being Kani Yoshinaga – Article 55
1554–1613; an excellent spear fighter and student of Inei, the founder of Hozo-ryu, a school of spear fighting. He served eight lords, the last being Fukushima Masanori. In the Battle of Sekigahara, he captured seventeen heads and was highly praised by Tokugawa Ieyasu.

Satake Yoshiaki – Article 48
1531–1565; the seventeenth lord of the Satake clan in Hitachi province. He died at the age of 34 just before he unified Hitachi province.

Shibui Naizen – Article 35
?–1614; a chief retainer to Satake Yoshishige. He was killed in the Winter Siege of Osaka Castle in 1614.

Shinagawa Okami-no-suke Masakazu – Article 56
1544–1565; a retainer of the Masuda clan and a provincial landlord in Iwami province. 'Okami' means 'wolf'. He was commonly called so in opposition to Yamanaka Shika-no-suke, as 'shika' means deer. He was extremely good at archery and had enormous strength. At the Battle of Gassan, which was a fight over Toda Castle, he met with Shika-no-suke in single combat and was killed by him at the age of 21.

Soma Daizen-no-kami Toshitane – Article 43
1581–1625; the son of Soma Yoshitane and the first daimyo of Soma Nakamura province.

Soma Daizen-no-sho Yoshitane – Article 43
1548-1635; the sixteenth inheritor of the Soma clan.

Sue Owari-no-kami Takafusa – Article 27
1521-55; a retainer of the Ouchi clan. He raised a rebellion against Ouchi Yoshitaka, as a result Yoshitaka Ouchi killed himself in 1551. He also fought with Mouri Motonari at the Battle of Itsukushima and was defeated so, killed himself in 1555.

Susukida Hayato-no-suke Kanesuke – Article 46 and 56
?-1615; a retainer of Kobayakawa Takagage. After being a knight errant, he joined the Toyotomi side at the Sieges of Osaka Castle, serving Toyotomi Hideyori, where he was killed in the Summer Siege.

Takagi (also, Honda) Kyusuke Hiromasa – Article 33
1536-1606; a retainer of Tokugawa Ieyasu. He defended Oshi Castle in Musashi province at the time of the Battle of Sekigahara and was given 3,000 koku for this victory.

Takayama Minami-no-bo Sakon – Article 30
1552-1615; famous as a Christian daimyo, he became the lord of Takatsuki Castle and later, after Nobunaga's death, served Hideyoshi and was given a fief of 60,000 koku in Harima province. However, with the order of abandonment of Christianity issued by Hideyoshi, he chose to give up his position as daimyo and lived in Kaga by favour of Maeda Toshiie and belonged to the army of the Maeda clan. In 1614, upon the Order of Deportation of the Christians by Tokugawa shogunage, he went to Manila, in the Philippines, and soon after died there.

Takeda Shingen Harunobu – Articles 7, 15, 21, 24, 31, 33, 38 and 57
1521-1573; a Sengoku daimyo of Kai province and nineteenth inheritor of the Takeda clan. Vastly famous as *the* greatest sovereign and most excellent general of the Sengoku period, a reputation largely revivd from the manuscript *Koyo Gunkan*, which was a popular war chronicle of the exploits of the Takeda clan. On top of Kai, he kept expanding his territory to include the provinces Shinano, Kozuke, Totoumi, part of Suruga and part of Mino. He died from disease during the Battle of Mikatagahara, and his death was kept secret for three years, as was in accordance with his will.

Takeda Katsuyori – Articles 38 and 57
1546-1582; the fourth son of Takeda Shingen and twentieth inheritor of
the Takeda clan. In the ambition to expand their territory more than his
father, he aggressively went on campaigns against the alliance of Oda and
Tokugawa. However, he suffered a catastrophic defeat at the Battle of
Nagashinoin in 1575, after this his power waned and he was killed in the
Battle of Tenmokuzan by the alliance of Oda and Tokugawa.

Tanaka Hyobu-no-tayu Yoshimasa – Article 20
1548-1609; he served Hideyoshi's son, Hideyori, and after Hideyori's
downfall, served Tokugawa Ieyasu. At the Battle of Sekigahara, he fought
for the East side and his men succeeded in the capture of the enemy
leader, Ishida Mitsunari. For this he was given Chikugo province with a
fief of 320,000 koku. He died from disease at the age of 62.

Tanaka Denzaemon – Article 20
Unknown dates; a retainer of Tanaka Yoshimasa.

Tokugawa Hidetada – Article 25
1579-1632; the third son of Tokugawa Ieyasu and the second Tokugawa
shogun of a then united Japan. Compared with his father and brothers,
his military ability is said to have been lower, however he secured the
foundation of the future of the shogunate.

Tokugawa Ieyasu – Articles 3, 10, 24, 30, 33, 39, 42, 50 and 57
1543-1616; founder and the first shogun of the Tokugawa regime and
final unifier of Japan and probably the most famous samurai in history,
alongside Miyamoto Musashi. Born in a comparatively weak landlord
family in the province of Mikawa, he spent his early days as a hostage with the Oda clan and then the Imagawa clan. After the Battle of
Okehazama, he became independent and allied himself with Nobunaga.
With this alliance, he destroyed the Takeda clan and taking advantage of
the confusion after the Honnoji Incident (Nobunaga's death), he secured
five provinces. Though he was always a competitor of Hideyoshi, he
became a retainer of Hideyoshi as a formality. However, after the death of
Hideyoshi, he destroyed the opposition forces in the Battle of Sekigahara
– the largest and greatest samurai battle – and ruined the inheritance of
the Toyotomi clan at the Summer and Winter Seiges of Osaka Castle,

at which point he fully unified Japan and founded the Tokugawa shogunate. He died from disease at the age of 75.

Tomita Kohei – Article 30
Unknown dates; a retainer of Niwa Nagashige.

Tomita Kurouzu Takasada – Article 30
?-1600; a retainer of Toyotomi Hidetsugu and Toyotomi Hideyoshi's stepson. But after Hidetsugu's fall, he went into service with the Maeda clan and was killed in the Battle of Daijoji in 1600.

Torii Shirozaemon Nobuyuki – Article 56
?-1573; a retainer of Tokugawa Ieyasu. In the Battle of Mikatagahara against Takeda Shingen, when Tokugawa's forces retreated, he fought at the rear of the retreat so that they could successfully withdraw. He was killed in this encounter.

Toyotomi Hideyoshi – Articles 4 and 20
1537-1598; born into a 'lower' family in Owari he served Oda Nobunaga and distinguished himself as capable and became one of the most trusted retainers of Nobunaga. After the assassination of Nobunaga, he destroyed Akechi Mitsuhide, the rebel who killed Nobunaga, and succeeded Nobunaga in position as head warlord of Japan and started to bring an end to the Sengoku, or warring, period. He conducted an invasion of Korea in 1592 to 1598 and during the middle of the second invasion, Hideyoshi died and his forces withdrew.

Toyotomi Hideyori – Articles 14, 35 and 46
1593-1615; son of Toyotomi Hideyoshi and born when Hideyoshi was 57 years old, he inherited the Toyotomi administration of Japan after his father's death in 1598. However, Tokugawa Ieyasu, while seizing more and more power after the Battle of Sekigahara, took the role of supreme ruler of Japan and later conducted the famous Sieges of Osaka Castle – in denial of his own promise to protect Hideyori. In the Summer Siege in 1615, Hideyori and his mother committed seppuku in Osaka Castle.

Tsuchiya Yemon-no-jo Masatsugu – Article 56
1544-1575; a retainer of Takeda Shingen and Takeda Katsuyori. He killed Torii Nobuyuki in the Battle of Mikatagahara in 1573 and he himself was killed in the Battle of Nagashino in 1575.

Tsukuda Mataemon – Article 17
?-1617; served Gamo Ujisato and later Fukushima Masanori. He was also a Christian. With the ban on Christianity issued in 1614, he refused to convert from his religion but Tokugawa Ieyasu gave him a pardon as he was a distinguished warrior. However, he kept true to his faith and gave Christians shelter and was thus executed in 1617.

Ueda Mondo-no-suke Shigeyasu – Article 56
1563-1650; first served the Niwa clan. After Niwa's fall, he served Toyotomi Hideyoshi. After the Battle of Sekigahara, went into service for the Asano clan. As well as numerous military achievements, he was famous as a garden designer and tea master.

Uesaka Shume – Article 30
Unknown dates; all that is known is found in Article 30.

Uesugi (also, Nagao) Kenshin – Articles 22, 31 and 54
1530-1578; the warlord of Echigo province. Famous for his bravery in warfare and thus called a 'god of war'. He unified Echigo and successfully promoted industry in his territory. He had numerous battles through his life against Takeda Shingen, Hojo Ujiyasu, Oda Nobunaga and many others, he famously fought on five occasions with Takeda Shingen at Kawanakajima in Shinano. He died suddenly from a disease while preparing for his next campaign.

Wada Yoshimori – Article 10
1147-1213; the military commander of the Kamakura shogunate. After Minamoto-no-Yoritomo's death, the Kamakura shogunate had a struggle for power with the Hojo clan and Yoshimori was killed in 1213, together with his family.

Yagi Shinzaemon – Article 56
Unknown dates; an ashigaru foot soldier for Asano Saemon, who was in turn a retainer of Asano Nagamasa.

Yamada Gorozaemon – Article 61
Unknown date; a ronin of Harima province. He joined the Toyotomi side in the Siege of Osaka Castle.

Yamaguchi Genba-no-kami Munenaga – Articles 30 and 50
?-1600; lord of Daijoji Castle in Kaga province. Sided with Ishida in the Battle of Sekigahara. In 1600 his castle was besieged by 20,000 men of the Maeda Toshimaga's forces while the besieged were only 500 in number. In the end he killed himself, together with his son.

Yamanaka Shika-no-suke Yukimori – Articles 41 and 56
1544-1578; born into the Amago clan, he was part of a very influential family in western Honshu. After 1566, when the Amago clan was ruined by the Mouri clan, he devoted himself to restore the clan, making three major attempts to reinstate it. Yamanaka served Oda Nobunaga and went against the Mouri clan, Yamanaka defended Kozuki Castle but surrendered it to the Mouri clan in the end. Yamanaka was captured alive but while he was being taken to the headquarters of the Mouri clan, he was killed by a retainer, as stated in Article 41.

Yamashita Matasuke – Article 13
Unknown dates; nothing is known of him except what is written in the above article.

Yamazaki Nagato-no-kami Naganori – Article 30
1552-1620; first served Asakura Yoshikage and after Asakura was ruined, he served Akechi Mitsuhide. After Akechi was killed, he served Shibata Katsuie, and after Shibata was killed by Hideyoshi, he served Maeda Toshiie and Toshinaga. Because he successfully ruined Yamaguchi Munenaga, he was given 12,000 koku by Maeda Toshinaga.

Yoshihiro Kahei-no-jo Muneyuki – Article 23
?-1600; a retainer to Otomo Yoshimune. He was killed at the Battle of Ishigakibara in 1600.

Watanabe Hanzo Moritsuna – Article 47
1542–1620; a retainer to Tokugawa Ieyasu. He is said that to have been good at spear fighting and fought in famous battles, such as the battles of Anegawa, Mikatagahara and Nagashino. Hence he was nicknamed Spear Hanzo and was included in the poem mentioned above, with Devil Hanzo and Head-Taker Gengo.

Bibliography

PRIMARY SOURCES

Musha Monogatari – the Japanese National Archives
Zoho-Monogatari – the Japanese National Archives

SECONDARY SOURCES

Kikuchi Shinichi & Nishimaru Keiko, *Musha Monogatari, Musha Monogatari Sho, Shin Musha, Monogatarai – Honbun to Sakuin*, Izumi Shoin, 1994
Kamo Yoshihisa, *Sinban Zohyo Monogatari*, Paroru Sha, 2006
Nakamura Michio, *Zohyo Monogatari, Oan Monogatari*, Iwanami Bunko, 1942
Asano Tagatake & Higuchi Hideo, *Zumaki, Zohyo Monogatari*, Jinbutsu Oraisha, 1967

Index